James Floyd Kelly

Sams **Teach Yourself**

Mint.com

in **10 Minutes**

SAMS | 800 East 96th Street, Indianapolis, Indiana 46240

Sams Teach Yourself Mint.com in 10 Minutes

ISBN-13: 978-0-672-33566-2

ISBN-10: 0-672-33566-2

Library of Congress Cataloging-in-Publication Data is on file

First Printing: August 2011

Trademarks

All terms mentioned in this book that are known to be trademarks or service marks have been appropriately capitalized. Pearson cannot attest to the accuracy of this information. Use of a term in this book should not be regarded as affecting the validity of any trademark or service mark.

Warning and Disclaimer

Every effort has been made to make this book as complete and as accurate as possible, but no warranty or fitness is implied. The information provided is on an "as is" basis. The author and the publisher shall have neither liability nor responsibility to any person or entity with respect to any loss or damages arising from the information contained in this book.

Bulk Sales

Pearson offers excellent discounts on this book when ordered in quantity for bulk purchases or special sales. For more information, please contact

    U.S. Corporate and Government Sales
    1-800-382-3419
    corpsales@pearsontechgroup.com

For sales outside of the U.S., please contact

    International Sales
    international@pearsoned.com

Executive Editor
Greg Wiegand

Acquisitions Editor
Laura Norman

Development Editor
Lora Baughey

Technical Editor
Christian Kenyeres

Managing Editor
Kristy Hart

Project Editor
Andy Beaster

Copy Editor
Barbara Hacha

Proofreader
Paula Lowell

Indexer
Erika Millen

Publishing Coordinator
Romny French

Book Designer
Gary Adair

Compositor
Nonie Ratcliff

Table of Contents

About the Author

James Floyd Kelly received an English degree from the University of West Florida and an Industrial Engineering degree from Florida State University; he has enjoyed using the skills and knowledge from both in various jobs over the years.

He is the author of numerous books, including books on the Galaxy Tab and Motorola Xoom tablets, building a CNC machine, building and programming LEGO robotics, and using open source software.

He currently lives with his wife and two sons in Atlanta, Georgia.

Dedication

For Mom and Dad—enjoy your retirement, and thank you for good examples of spending and saving.

Acknowledgments

I write books on many different topics, but it's always fun to write one that is relevant and useful to me personally and long term. When I discovered Mint.com and began using it, I quickly realized how much easier it made my life and how much time it freed up for other things. I'd like to thank Laura Norman for helping push the proposal for this book through and seeing Mint.com as I do—a great money-management tool that everyone should know about and take for a test spin.

I'd also like to thank Romny French and the rest of the Pearson crew who helped get this book prepared and out the door. Writing a book is hard work, but so is getting the author's words and figures into a presentable and useful form—thank you all for your hard work.

We Want to Hear from You

As the reader of this book, you are our most important critic and commentator. We value your opinion and want to know what we're doing right, what we could do better, what areas you'd like to see us publish in, and any other words of wisdom you're willing to pass our way.

You can email or write me directly to let me know what you did or didn't like about this book—as well as what we can do to make our books stronger.

Please note that I cannot help you with technical problems related to the topic of this book, and that due to the high volume of mail I receive, I might not be able to reply to every message.

When you write, please be sure to include this book's title and author, as well as your name and contact information. I will carefully review your comments and share them with the author and editors who worked on the book.

Email: consumer@samspublishing.com

Mail: Greg Wiegand
           Associate Publisher
           Sams Publishing
           800 East 96th Street
           Indianapolis, IN 46240 USA

Reader Services

Visit our website and register this book at informit.com/register for convenient access to any updates, downloads, or errata that might be available for this book.

Introduction

In today's high-speed, on-the-go world, the Internet intersects with just about every aspect of our lives. We communicate via email, schedule online appointments for medical and dental visits, download and listen to music, check our favorite teams' scores and schedules, upload pictures of our vacation, and so much more. Although we're aware of the risks involved with the Internet, the benefits easily outweigh the dangers, especially if we educate ourselves and keep informed.

Given that so much of our daily life activities involves the Internet in some way, it should come as no surprise that services exist that allow us to also manage our financial life via the Internet. We can trade stocks, buy car insurance, and open up a savings account all online, without ever stepping foot in a physical building.

But keeping track of our financial life can be just as crazy and confusing as any other activities in our lives. We end up with numerous usernames and passwords for all those online accounts we use to manage our checking accounts, savings accounts, credit cards, mortgage, car loan, investments, and more. There has to be a better way, right?

Well, fortunately Mint.com has already done the hard work for you. Mint.com has created a free online service that will help you manage all aspects of your financial life. By logging in to one website, you're given a snapshot of your current financial situation and the capability to dig deeper should you want to do so.

Mint.com is not a complicated service, but it can be a bit overwhelming at first with all the different questions it asks and information it requests. If you're looking for a guide to walk with you as you set up your Mint.com account, you've found the right book. Here's what you're going to learn:

▶ How Mint.com works and how it keeps your data secure

▶ How to view your checking and savings account balances and access all transactions

▶ How to monitor your credit card balances and view charges

▶ How Mint.com tracks your loans—car, home, and others

▶ How to watch your investments and track their performance

▶ How to configure Mint.com to communicate with you via text messages and emails and alert you to unusual activities

▶ How to use Mint.com to make and use a budget

▶ How Mint.com helps you set goals (such as a vacation or home purchase) and then reach them

▶ How Mint.com can find you better deals on credit card and savings account interest rates and more

▶ How to access your Mint.com account via mobile devices such as phones and tablets

▶ How to link up with other Mint.com users in the forums and find answers to your questions

You'll learn about these services and more and see how Mint.com's features and tools can simplify your financial life, freeing up time for other activities.

Who Is This Book For?

This book is for you if

▶ You are looking for an easier way to monitor all aspects of your financial life.

▶ You want an online financial management service but are concerned about security.

▶ You want step-by-step walkthroughs of the most popular and useful features of Mint.com.

▶ You'd like to understand what services and tools Mint.com offers before actually signing up and trying them out.

Conventions Used in This Book

I'll be providing additional material in each lesson that may be useful to some Mint.com users but not everyone. This new information is provided in the form of boxes as described next:

> NOTE: A note presents interesting pieces of information related to the surrounding discussion.

> TIP: A tip offers advice or teaches an easier way to do something.

> CAUTION: A caution advises you about potential problems and helps you steer clear of disaster.

LESSON 1

Mint.com Overview

This lesson gives you an overview of Mint.com's basic features and services that are covered in more detail later in the book. You also see the process for creating a Mint.com user account, linking a credit card or bank account, and making your user account more secure.

What Is Mint.com?

It seems today that almost everything related to your personal financial situation has a digital version. If you have a checkbook, you likely have an online banking account that you can use to view your balance, transfer funds, and even look at scanned images of your outstanding checks.

If you have any investments, it's likely that you receive monthly statements in the mail that keep you informed about the ups and downs of the markets.

And if you have a loan—mortgage, car, or maybe even educational—you know how important it is to make payments on time and to be able to check the status of the loan, including information such as the loan APR, the balance due, and how much of your monthly payment applies to the principal and how much goes to the interest.

Checking and savings accounts. Car loans. Home mortgages. Credit cards. Investments. They're all crucial and important services that require tracking, making payments and deposits, transferring funds, and checking balances. Each and every one of them typically requires a separate username and password to log in to a secure website to access the information. The more financial services you use, the more websites, usernames, and passwords you must manage.

It's not uncommon for people to spend hours each week monitoring all their financial activities, scattered over numerous websites. We all want to have better control and a more detailed knowledge of our financial life, but it shouldn't have to be so time consuming and tedious.

It shouldn't have to be—and it isn't. Because Mint.com (see Figure 1.1) is your secret weapon for consolidating all your financial services—checking, loans, credit cards, and more—into a single, easy-to-remember website that guards your information with strong security, puts access to all your financial accounts on a single page, and offers you the capability to find better deals (better credit card rates, lower APR rates for automobile purchases, and more).

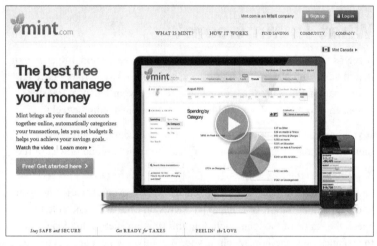

FIGURE 1.1   Mint.com is a single-source financial management website.

Oh, and Mint.com charges no fees. Zero. How's that for a good financial incentive to keep reading?

Mint.com has an extremely short explanation on its home page that summarizes its primary purpose:

"Mint brings all your financial accounts together online, automatically categorizes your transactions, lets you set budgets & helps you achieve your savings goals."

Behind that simple statement, however, there's a lot going on.

Financial Overview

Mint.com pulls in all the account data (that you choose to authorize) from your various financial institutions: banking, investments, loans, and credit cards. It sifts this information, behind the scenes, and presents it to you in a more easily understandable format with nothing more than a web browser (or a smartphone app—more on that later in Lesson 11, "Mint.com Mobile Versions") and an Internet connection. This means that no matter where you are—at work or home or even a friend's house—you can view all your financial information with a single URL, www.mint.com.

Have you ever received a printed financial statement in the mail that looked like it could confuse the most experienced accountant? If so, you can appreciate the simplicity of Mint.com's user interface that we'll cover shortly. Mint.com is capable of taking all your financial records and consolidating and merging them into a single web page that provides an easy-to-follow summary of your current financial situation—money coming in and money going out. Figure 1.2 shows a portion of the Overview user interface page that displays financial information categories: Cash, Credit Cards, Loans, Investments, Property, and Net Worth. (The last two become visible when you scroll down the web page a bit.)

Stick to a Budget

Another key feature that Mint.com offers to users is the capability to create and monitor a budget. (Mint.com pulls down all your linked financial data so you'll always be able to go back and reference historical financial data at any time, even if your financial institutions only allow you to go back three or six months, for example.) After you create a budget, Mint.com does all the work for you by locating your expenses (from credit card and checking account records) and itemizing them under the Budget screen shown in Figure 1.3.

Save Money

In addition to the budget feature, Mint.com also strives to help its users find ways to save more money (including increasing their investments).

FIGURE 1.2   The Overview page summarizes all your financial information.

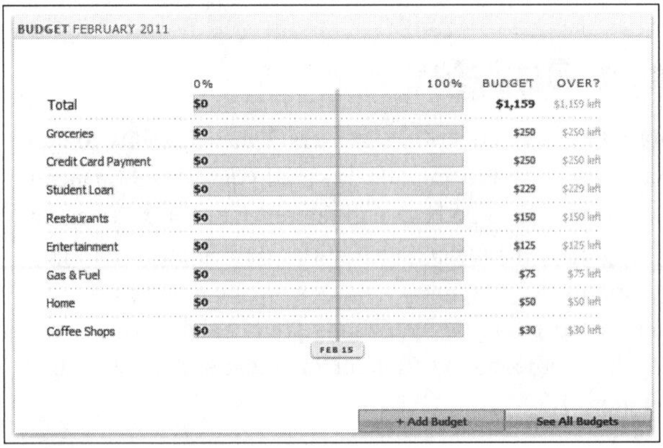

FIGURE 1.3   Create a budget to help you track where your money goes.

As mentioned earlier, Mint.com doesn't charge its users any fees. It's truly 100% free with no strings attached. So if you're wondering how Mint.com makes money and stays in business, the short answer is that Mint.com points you to businesses that can save you money and receives fees from these organizations if you choose to accept an offer. This includes credit card companies, banks, and mortgage firms that offer lower interest rates, but there are many more money saving options that you'll learn about later in the book.

Figure 1.4 shows an area of the Mint.com user interface that provides you with links to companies and services that can help you find better deals on auto loans, credit cards, checking accounts, and more.

FIGURE 1.4   Mint.com finds you ways to save even more money.

Mint.com doesn't hit you with pop-up advertisements and in-your-face promotions that irritate most users. Instead, it offers you the links shown in Figure 1.4 that take you to pages that explain in more detail how you can save money.

For example, Figure 1.4 indicates you can save more than $2,000.00 in the Banking category. If you click this link, you are given a list of credit card companies that are willing to transfer any outstanding balance(s) on your credit card(s) to a card with a lower interest rate.

> NOTE: **Your Savings May Vary**
>
> The savings values calculated by Mint.com are based on your own unique situation, such as your existing credit card's minimum monthly payment and interest rate, so you may see a higher or lower savings value than the ones shown here.

Spot Trends

In addition to saving you money, Mint.com can also help identify trends. These could be in areas of spending, saving, or even investment. Figure 1.5 shows a portion of the user interface screen where you can view quick summaries of trends that Mint com has identified. In this example, a large credit card debit has been identified that doesn't match previous months' spending. This could alert you to possible credit card fraud or simply remind you that the treadmill in your basement is still waiting for your daily 30-minute run. You can receive these alerts from the Overview page or via text or email alerts that you'll learn how to configure in Lesson 6, "Alerts."

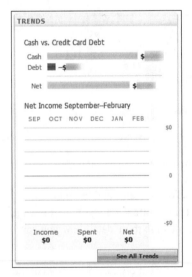

FIGURE 1.5   Mint.com excels at spotting trends both in saving and spending.

Details, Details

Every feature on Mint.com's Overview page offers you the capability to dig deeper and view more detailed information. For example, the Trends category shown in Figure 1.5 offers a link to See All Trends. When you click it, you can view specific trends (on a monthly basis or a month-to-month, side-by-side comparison, for example), such as Net Income or Spending Overtime, as shown in Figure 1.6. Hey, look at that! You managed to save almost $800 in February.

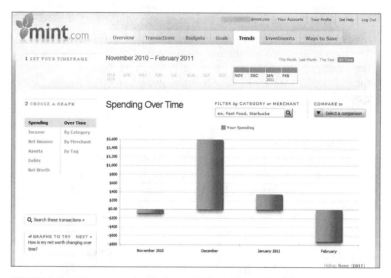

FIGURE 1.6 View more detailed trend information, including over time.

The Overview page may very well be the only page you ever need to visit. For many Mint.com users, the Overview page provides just the right amount of information and keeps all the nitty-gritty details hidden from view.

One-Click Tool Tabs

Most Mint.com users are going to want to dig deeper every now and then to see what's really going on behind the curtain when it comes to their spending, savings, and investments. That's why Mint.com offers a set of tool tabs along the top of the Overview page that allow you to view more detailed information but be only a single click away from jumping back to the Overview page. Figure 1.7 shows the tabs available: Overview, Transactions, Budgets, Goals, Trends, Investments, and Ways to Save.

FIGURE 1.7   Tabs hide the details but give one-click access to more information.

NOTE: **Avoiding Information Overload**

Mint.com is all about making your financial data understandable. The tabs offered are not the only features available, but they are the most popular. You learn all about the features behind these tabs in later lessons, including features not so prominently displayed.

For example, clicking the Transactions tab provides you with a list of all your various accounts (checking, savings, investments) down the left side of the screen. If you click one of the accounts, the details are displayed, front and center, or you can select All Accounts, as shown in Figure 1.8.

FIGURE 1.8   Account details tell you where the money is going.

Mint.com is extremely user friendly, too. The Account Details screen in Figure 1.8 may look a bit complicated, but it's the exception, not the rule. For example, Figure 1.9 shows the Goals tab. It's an icon-driven tool that allows you to specify what you want to do. Buy a car? Click the button. Make some home improvements? Click the button. The Goals tab and its buttons will walk you through steps that allow you to specify costs, create a budget, track your savings, and even offer relevant companies that can finance the more expensive projects you may have.

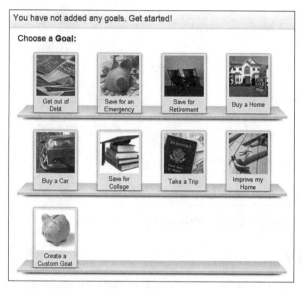

You have not added any goals. Get started!

Choose a **Goal:**

Get out of Debt

Save for an Emergency

Save for Retirement

Buy a Home

Buy a Car

Save for College

Take a Trip

Improve my Home

Create a Custom Goal

FIGURE 1.9 Create goals that can be tracked and funded through savings or financing.

The Mint.com Community

This book helps you get up to speed quickly, but there may come a time when you have a more specific question or need assistance with the Mint.com tools.

It's good to know that the Mint.com community of users is large and helpful. The Mint.com forum provides access to more than 150,000 registered users and more than 50 actual Mint.com employees. You can search the forum for answers to your questions and, if you don't find what you need, post your own question.

Figure 1.10 shows the basic Mint.com forum where you can post questions, make suggestions for improving the Mint.com services, and view answers to the most common problems Mint.com users may encounter.

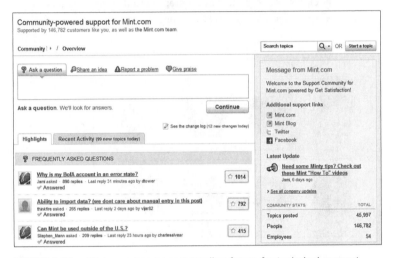

FIGURE 1.10 Mint.com has an outstanding forum for technical support.

Security

Mint.com has great services, but no one would use them if they didn't come with some outstanding security. No one wants their personal financial data to be viewed by strangers, and Mint.com provides the same level of data security used in the banking and financial sectors.

Figure 1.11 shows several badges that are prominently displayed at the bottom of the Overview page, but what do they actually mean?

FIGURE 1.11 Mint.com takes the security of your data seriously.

Before you sign up to use Mint.com (covered later in this lesson), take a moment to click the How We Keep You Safe link just above the icons in Figure 1.11.

You are taken to a page that Mint.com has created to address the concerns of its users. What you learn is that Mint.com uses the same type of data encryption provided by banks; it doesn't allow the person logged in to move money around; and your user account can be created to protect your real identity (name). Mint.com also provides the capability to configure alerts that will let you know when suspicious activity has been detected; you'll read more on that in Lesson 6.

NOTE: **Read Mint.com's Privacy Statement**

Click the Privacy & Security link shown in Figure 1.11 to read Mint.com's security/privacy statements. It's important that you understand what Mint.com will and will not do with your information. If you read it carefully, you see that Mint.com isn't really interested in your financial information—only in keeping it secure and away from prying eyes.

Sign Up

Mint.com offers some great features and services, but none of them are available to you until you sign up and create a user account. If you're ready to give Mint.com a try (there are no contracts—you can quit and delete your account any time you want), point a web browser to www. mint.com and click the Sign Up button, as shown in Figure 1.12.

FIGURE 1.12   Give your Mint.com account a strong password.

You are asked to provide an email address, country, ZIP code, and a password, as shown in Figure 1.13. (Enter the email address and password twice.)

FIGURE 1.13 Provide some basic information to create your account.

Place a check in the box to agree to Mint.com's Terms of Use and click the Sign Up button.

NOTE: **Choose a Strong Password**

Mint.com is going to provide financial details to the person logged in. Make certain no one else can access this information by choosing a strong password. A strong password will contain a mixture of uppercase and lowercase letters, one or more numbers, and special characters. Create a password that is hard to guess and don't write it down where someone could find it. Someone logged in to your account may not be able to transfer money or make purchases, but it's not a good idea to let someone even view this information without your permission. Be smart and choose a good, strong password for your Mint.com account.

To complete your Mint.com user account, you need to link it to either a credit card or a bank account, as shown in Figure 1.14. Search for a bank or credit card name or select it from the list of common names.

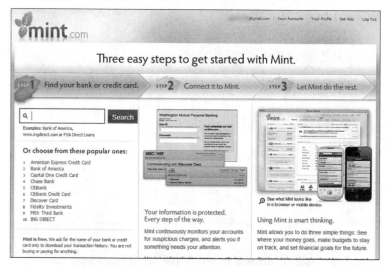

FIGURE 1.14 Add a credit card or bank to your Mint.com account.

Depending on whether you select a bank or credit card, a window will appear, like the one in Figure 1.15, that will walk you through providing the right information. Figure 1.15 shows that the American Express credit card has been found.

Depending on whether you chose a credit card or bank, you need to provide information such as a username and password or account number to create the link between Mint.com and the chosen account. Figure 1.16 shows that I've provided my username and password that are linked to my American Express account.

Click the Add It! button and the linking process begins. Figure 1.17 shows that Mint.com was successful in linking to my American Express account and that I have a current balance of $68.05. Above that notice you see that

I can also choose at this time to add my bank account. I'm going to skip that for now by clicking the Close button and show you how to do it in Lesson 2, "Checking and Savings Accounts." (Down the left side of Figure 1.17 you see other types of accounts I can link to Mint.com—more on these in later lessons.)

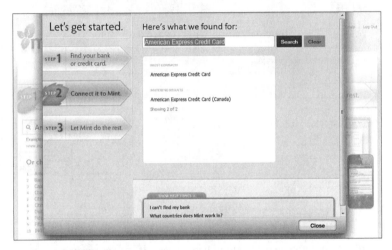

FIGURE 1.15   Find the correct credit card or bank name.

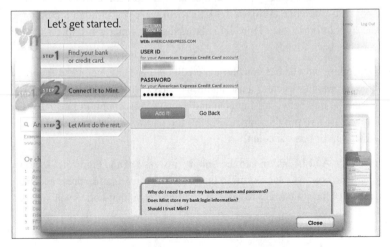

FIGURE 1.16   Provide username and password information if requested.

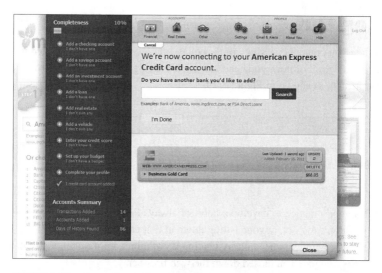

FIGURE 1.17   A credit card has been linked to Mint.com.

After clicking the Close button, the Overview page will be displayed as shown in Figure 1.18. It doesn't have a lot of information right now, but that will all change after a few bank accounts, a mortgage, a car loan, and other financial details are added (in later lessons).

FIGURE 1.18   The Overview page with a credit card account added.

Log Out

When you create your Mint.com account, you are automatically logged in to Mint.com. For now, go ahead and click the Log Out button at the top of the screen, as shown in Figure 1.19.

FIGURE 1.19   Log out of your Mint.com account.

It's a good practice to develop a habit of always logging out of Mint.com. If you don't log out, anyone sitting down at that computer may be able to view your Mint.com account by visiting www.mint.com if not enough time has passed since you closed down the web browser.

The next time you want to access your Mint.com account, point your browser to www.mint.com and click the Log In button in the upper-right corner (see Figure 1.20).

FIGURE 1.20   Log in to Mint.com with your email and password.

Figure 1.20 shows you the Log In screen, where you always need to provide your email address and password. Enter that information, click the Log In button, and you are taken to the Overview screen.

Summary

In this lesson you learned some of the basic features of Mint.com, including how it helps monitor your spending, savings, and investments. You learned about Mint.com's security, set up your Mint.com account, and linked a bank or credit card account.

Checking and Savings Accounts

In this lesson, you learn how to link both checking and savings accounts to your Mint.com account. You also learn how to remove an account.

Your Checking Account

Back in Lesson 1, "Mint.com Overview," you created your Mint.com account and linked it with a single credit card. It's a good start, but as you can see in Figure 2.1, the Overview page is not too helpful right now with information—you see lots of $0.00 placeholders waiting for real values. Many categories need to be set up, including checking, savings, investments, and loans, such as car or mortgage.

One of the first tasks you should consider when configuring your Mint.com account is linking it with your personal checking account. This serves many purposes.

It allows you to view funds coming in and out. Although you can easily log in to your bank's online checking website to see whether a check has cleared or a deposit has gone through, it's going to be so much easier to allow Mint.com to gather this information for you and present it alongside other financial information, such as your home mortgage balance, credit card balance(s), and even how you're doing following a budget.

Linking to your checking account also allows you to itemize your purchases (using categories—more on this later) so you can more easily view where your money is going each month. Is it spent on food? Is a large percentage of your money going toward entertainment? What percentage of your monthly paycheck is going toward retirement?

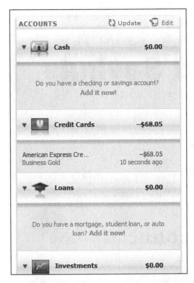

FIGURE 2.1   Mint.com's Summary section is mostly empty at first.

Many financial planners agree that knowing your spending habits and where your money is going each month is one of the first steps to gaining control of spending and making smarter decisions.

So, let's get a personal checking account linked to your Mint.com account. Figure 2.2 shows that the Cash category on the Overview page shows a value of $0.00. The term *cash* is simply defined here as how much money is sitting in checking and savings accounts. After bills are paid and deposits are made, this is likely going to be a very important value that you frequently check when you log in to Mint.com.

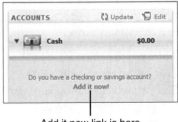

Add it now link is here

FIGURE 2.2   Add a checking account to change that $0.00 value.

Linking Checking to Mint.com

There are two easy ways to link your personal checking account to
Mint.com. The first is to click the Add It Now! link under the Cash category (see Figure 2.2). The other is to click the Your Accounts link in the
upper-right corner of the screen, as shown in Figure 2.3.

Your Accounts link here

FIGURE 2.3   You can link a checking account to Mint.com using the Your
Accounts link.

No matter which of the two methods you use to link a checking account,
you are taken to the screen shown in Figure 2.4. This screen may look
familiar to you from Lesson 1. Know that anytime you want to link any
type of financial account, you can always click Your Accounts to get to
this screen.

Notice in Figure 2.4 that Mint.com gives you an estimated Completeness
percentage based on how much financial information you've provided.
Figure 2.4 shows a value of 10%. This will change as you add more
accounts to Mint.com.

Now it's time to link a checking account, and Mint.com has made it as
easy as browsing down the left side of the screen in Figure 2.4 to locate
the Add a Checking Account option at the very top of the list. Click that
option and you can either enter the name of your bank in the search field,
as shown in Figure 2.5, or select a bank name from a list of popular banks
below the search field.

If you use the search field, click the Search button. If your bank name is
similar to other bank names, you may be given a list of possible matches
to choose from, as shown in Figure 2.6.

Click your bank from the list of options and you are presented with a
screen like the one shown in Figure 2.7, requesting the User ID and password that you use when logging in to your bank's online banking website.

FIGURE 2.4 Your Accounts screen where you link accounts.

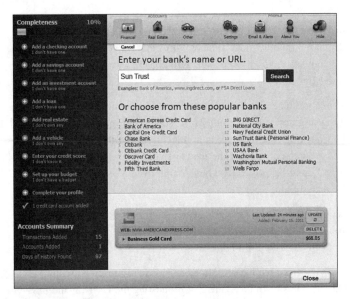

FIGURE 2.5 Search for your bank or select it from the list.

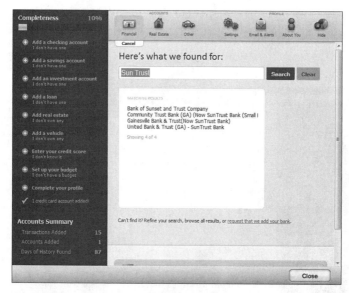

FIGURE 2.6   Select your bank if given a list of possible options.

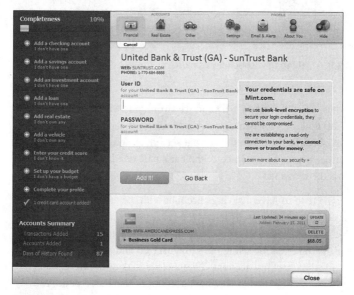

FIGURE 2.7   Provide a user ID and password for your checking account.

After entering your user ID and password, click the Add It! button. You may see a screen telling you to wait as the account is checked and linked, as shown in Figure 2.8.

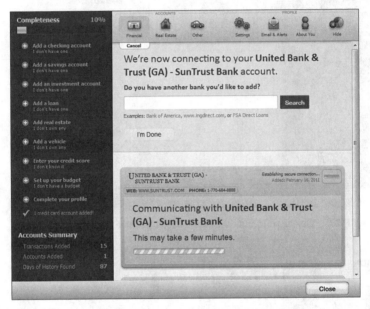

FIGURE 2.8   Linking to a checking account may take a few minutes.

If you entered the correct user ID and password, and Mint.com is able to successfully link to your bank, you should see your bank's name and your current balance displayed on the current screen, as shown in Figure 2.9. (If you've already linked a credit card, the bank name and balance should be listed directly above it.)

Most people tend to have a savings account with the same bank they use for their checking accounts. If this is the case, you won't need to go through the steps to add a savings account because Mint.com will be able to gather that information using the same user ID and password that you supplied for the checking account. Take a close look at Figure 2.9 and you see that a money market (savings) account is also listed under the bank name.

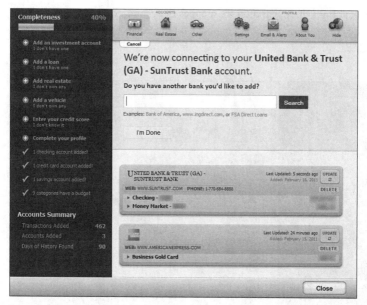

FIGURE 2.9 A checking account linked to Mint.com.

Your Savings Account

If you want to link a savings account to your Mint.com account, you also have three alternatives.

The first is to click the Add It Now! link on the Overview page (see Figure 2.2). This option is available only if you have not already set up a checking account. After a checking account has been linked, the Add It Now! option goes away.

The second method is to click the Your Accounts link (see Figure 2.3) and then click Add a Savings Account (see Figure 2.4).

The process for adding a savings account is identical to the previously described method for linking to a checking account. You search for the bank's name, provide a user ID and password, and then let Mint.com set up the link.

The third method is a bit different and is required only if you've already linked both a checking and savings account to Mint.com. Because the shortcut links disappear after these types of accounts are added, you need to add a new account by clicking once on the Financial tab shown in Figure 2.10.

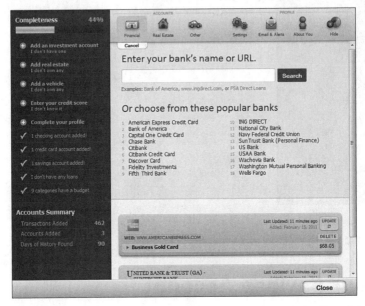

FIGURE 2.10   Add more checking or savings accounts with the Financial tab.

Enter the name of the bank or financial institution in the search field, as shown in Figure 2.11, click the Search button, and then select the name if a list of possible organizations is provided.

Depending on the organization and account type, you are asked to provide some type of authorization. For checking and savings accounts, it's often a user ID and password, but as you can see in Figure 2.12, sometimes the requested information goes by different names. (In this case, Mint.com is requesting a Customer Number/Saver ID and an Access Code.)

After you provide the requested information and click the Add It! button, Mint.com attempts to authenticate the account and then list it with your other accounts, as shown in Figure 2.13.

FIGURE 2.11 Provide the name of another financial institution.

FIGURE 2.12 Provide the required credentials for another account.

Click the Close button at the bottom of the screen (see Figure 2.13) and
you are returned to the Overview tab. Examine the Overview tab carefully;
you should see all checking and savings accounts listed under the Cash
category in the left column, as shown in Figure 2.14.

FIGURE 2.13   Another account added to Mint.com.

FIGURE 2.14   Checking and savings accounts under the Cash category on
the Overview tab.

Deleting an Account

People change banks every day, closing checking and savings accounts and opening new ones. Mint.com makes it simple to delete an account.

First, click the Your Accounts link in the upper-right corner of the screen (refer to Figure 2.3). Your accounts are divided among three tabs running across the top of the screen shown in Figure 2.15: Financial, Real Estate, and Other. (The Real Estate and Other tabs are discussed in later lessons, but the one you're interested in right now is the Financial tab.)

FIGURE 2.15 You can find accounts under one of three tabs.

Click the Financial tab (it should be selected by default, but click it if you're on a different tab). You may have to scroll down the window that appears in Figure 2.16 to view all your accounts (savings, checking, investment).

FIGURE 2.16 View all the accounts under the Financial tab.

Locate the account that you want to remove from Mint.com and click the Delete button to the right of the account's name, as shown in Figure 2.17.

FIGURE 2.17   Use the Delete button to remove an account.

A confirmation window appears, like the one shown in Figure 2.18. If you're certain you want to remove the account, type **DELETE** into the text field and click the Okay button. Otherwise, click Cancel.

FIGURE 2.18   Delete an account to remove it from the Overview page.

If you choose to delete the account, after clicking the Okay button, you are returned to the Your Accounts page, and the selected account will no longer appear in the list, as shown in Figure 2.19.

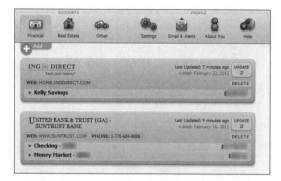

FIGURE 2.19   A deleted account is removed from the Financial tab.

Summary

In this lesson you learned how to add checking and savings accounts to your Mint.com account. You learned multiple methods for adding accounts as well as how to remove an account from Mint.com.

LESSON 3

Credit Cards

In this lesson, you learn how to link up credit cards to your Mint.com account. You also learn how to use Mint.com to view account information on credit cards and other types of accounts.

Your Credit Card(s)

In Lesson 1, "Mint.com Overview," you created your Mint.com account and were asked to make an initial link to either a bank account (checking or savings) or a credit card. You may have chosen to add a credit card at that time, so feel free to skip this first section and jump to the "View Credit Card Details" section.

However, if you added a checking or savings account initially, you likely do not have a credit card linked to your Mint.com account yet. Figure 3.1 shows the Overview page with the Credit Card category empty.

Many people have multiple credit cards, and Mint.com easily allows a user to add as many credit cards as needed. If you are a person who charges up your cards each month and then pays them off with a single payment monthly, you can expect to see the Credit Card category (see Figure 3.1) fluctuate quite a bit. This, in turn, will cause other parts of Mint.com to fluctuate because your credit card balances are treated as debt and affect things such as your overall net worth and any budgets you set. But if you want to use Mint.com to its fullest, and gain a better understanding of your financial situation, you need to update your Mint.com account with every credit card you have. Fortunately, Mint.com makes it extremely simple to link multiple credit cards.

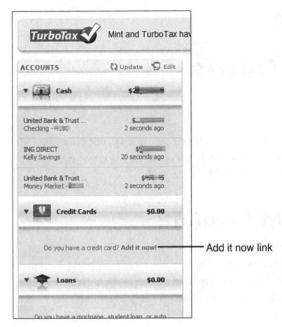

FIGURE 3.1   Mint.com's Overview page shows an empty Credit Card category.

Linking a Credit Card to Mint.com

You can use two methods to link credit cards to Mint.com. The first, as you can see in Figure 3.1, is to click the Add It Now! link. The other method is to click Your Accounts in the upper-right corner of the screen. Both methods will take you to the screen shown in Figure 3.2.

If you've added a checking or savings account already, this screen will be quite familiar to you. You start by typing in the name of the credit card—most likely the name of the financial institution will be printed on the front of the credit card and easy to find.

Figure 3.3 shows that I'm going to search for American Express, a well-known credit card company. I type the name into the search field and click the Search button.

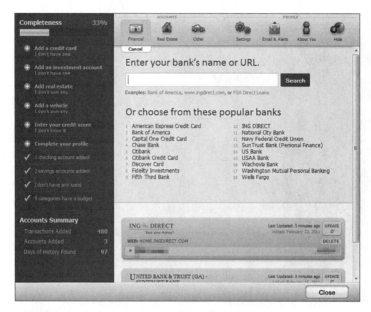

FIGURE 3.2 Adding a credit card is a simple task.

Mint.com provides you with a short list of possible matches. Pay careful attention to the names shown in the list, because banks often use common words in their names: First National, Commerce, and Trust are some examples.

Figure 3.3 shows that Mint.com has identified four possible matches. It provides the Most Common credit card first (and that's the one I want) as well as three other options.

NOTE: **You Can't Make a Mistake**

If you should accidentally click the wrong credit card link, don't worry—you won't be able to link it to Mint.com because you won't have the proper user ID and password required. Instead, cancel the linking task and start over. If you cannot find your credit card using the search feature, use the Request That We Add Your Bank link shown in Figure 3.3, and follow the instructions.

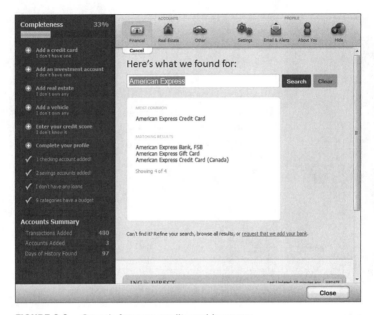

FIGURE 3.3   Search for your credit card by name.

After you click the correct credit card listing, you see a screen like the one shown in Figure 3.4, where you need to provide a user ID and password.

Type the user ID and password into the proper fields and click the Add It! button to create the link between Mint.com and your credit card.

Figure 3.5 shows that Mint.com is attempting to create the link by submitting your user ID and password to the credit card company.

If all goes well, the link is finalized and the credit card account is added to the bottom of the screen, along with your other accounts, as shown in Figure 3.6.

Click the Close button at the bottom of the window (see Figure 3.6) and you are returned to the Overview page. Notice in Figure 3.7 that any credit card balances you have are shown as a negative value. The negative lets you know that it's a debt; don't mistake it as a payment that you've made.

FIGURE 3.4   Provide a user ID and password to complete the link.

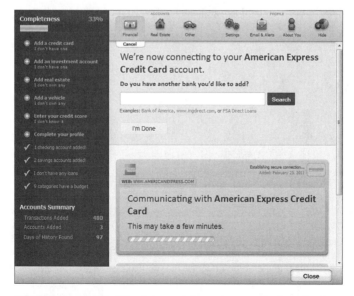

FIGURE 3.5   Creating the link can take up to one minute or longer.

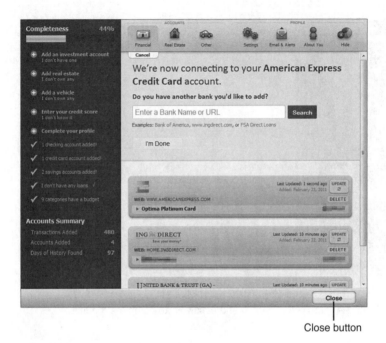

Close button

FIGURE 3.6   Your credit card is now linked to Mint.com.

Negative sign indicates a debt

FIGURE 3.7   A negative credit card value means you owe money on the card.

After you are linked to a single credit card, click the Your Accounts link in the upper-right corner of the screen to add any additional credit cards you want linked to your Mint.com account. Search for the name of your credit card as before, and follow the same process of selecting the correct card from the list of search results. Then provide a user ID and password, and let Mint.com create the link. Multiple credit cards are listed (by name) under the Credit Card category (see Figure 3.7).

View Credit Card Details

After your credit card is linked to Mint.com, you can easily view the account details, including purchases and payments made. To do so, move your mouse pointer over the name of the credit card. A line appears under the name, as shown in Figure 3.8. Click once on the name.

Selected card will be underlined

FIGURE 3.8   Select the credit card to view account details.

Next, you see a screen similar to the one in Figure 3.9. There is a lot of information here, but it's not difficult to understand.

Let's start with the top of the page, shown in Figure 3.10. Here you find the most basic information for your credit card: balance, available credit, total credit, and the APR. (Credit cards such as American Express that are paid in full monthly have an APR of 0.00%.)

FIGURE 3.9   Linked credit card details for viewing.

FIGURE 3.10   Basic credit card details are listed at the top.

Below the basic details, you see a listing of both credit card charges and credit card payments. Charges appear in black and payments appear in green. This information is organized using four columns: Date, Description, Category, and Amount.

Notice in Figure 3.10 that the Date tab has a downward pointing triangle. This indicates that the financial information is sorted chronologically, with the most recent charges listed first. Click the Date tab once and you see that the arrow now points upward, as shown in Figure 3.11. This sorts the information so that the oldest charge is at the top and the newest charge is at the bottom.

Click to sort Date column

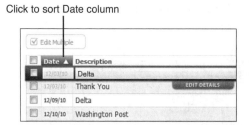

FIGURE 3.11 You can sort charges and payments by date.

The Description column typically provides the name of the company to which you charged a payment. Sometimes the name is vague or doesn't provide enough details, so Mint.com enables you to see more details on a charge. Click the name of a company (such as Delta), as shown in Figure 3.11, and click the Edit Details button to view more information related to the charge. Notice in Figure 3.12 that you can mark a charge as reimbursable, tax related, or vacation (more on using these tags shortly). You can also type in a note that helps you (or anyone else with access to your Mint.com account) make more sense of all your charges when you review them at a later time.

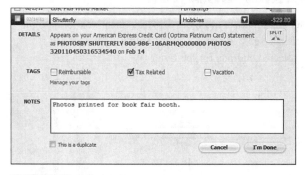

FIGURE 3.12 View hidden details on a credit card charge.

The Category column is another feature that you can easily change for a charge. If you select a charge as described earlier, instead of clicking the Edit Details button, click the small downward pointing triangle next to the charge's current Category listing and choose a different one from the drop-down menu, as shown in Figure 3.13.

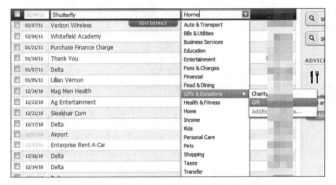

FIGURE 3.13 Change a charge's category using the drop-down menu.

Those are the most basic features available when viewing a credit card account screen, but there's much more that you can do from this screen.

View Similar Charges

Click a single charge, as shown in Figure 3.14, and then look to the right side of the screen. You see two new Show All buttons—one for the Description you selected and one for the Category.

Click to view similar items

FIGURE 3.14 View identical descriptions or categories.

Click one of the buttons (Show All Hobbies in this example), and you are given a shorter list of charges like the ones shown in Figure 3.15. This list will contain either charges that match the Description or the Category that you previously selected.

FIGURE 3.15 Charges that match the Hobbies category.

Click the Clear This Search button (see Figure 3.15) to return to the complete credit card list of charges and payments.

Use Tags

If you choose to use the check boxes shown in Figure 3.12 to mark a charge as reimbursable, tax related, or vacation, you can easily search for all charges that fit one of those categories, making it easy to provide an itemized listing of charges to an employer or tax preparer.

Click a tag, as shown in Figure 3.16, and any charges tagged with that selection are listed.

Mint.com gives you three preconfigured tags (Reimbursable, Tax Related, and Vacation), but you can easily modify these or even add your own. Click the Edit button next to the Tags category (see Figure 3.16), and you are presented with a window like the one in Figure 3.17.

Click a tag to filter charges

FIGURE 3.16   Sort using tags to find related charges.

Click to add
your own tag

FIGURE 3.17   Add a tag or modify an existing one.

Click the Add a New Tag button, type in a name, and click the Save button. Now, when you edit the details on a charge, you see your new tag as a box that can be checked, like the Book Related tag shown in Figure 3.18. Your new tag is added to the Tags category on the left side of the screen.

Your custom tag is listed

FIGURE 3.18   Use your own tags for sorting charges.

Export Your Data

Mint.com also allows you to export the financial data to a CSV file that can easily be imported into a spreadsheet or other financial planning software.

To do this, scroll to the bottom of the window and click the Export All X Transactions link, as shown in Figure 3.19.

Follow the onscreen instructions, and a file named transactions.csv is saved to your computer. You can open this CSV file with any spreadsheet or other financial software application that can import CSV files.

TIP: **You Can View Data but Not Change It**

Mint.com allows you to view all financial data gathered from other sources (banks, credit cards, and so on) and export it all to a CSV file. But Mint.com does not allow you to make changes to actual values (such as credit card charges or deposits made). Keep this in mind as you view your financial data. Any discrepancies you find will need to be addressed with the matching financial institution, not Mint.com.

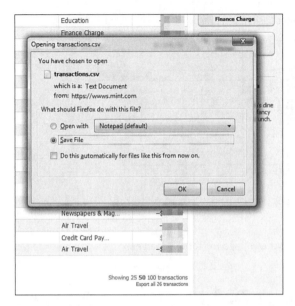

FIGURE 3.19   Export your data for use with other software.

View Other Accounts

As with credit cards, any other accounts linked to Mint.com can also have their details presented in a manner similar to what you've seen with credit cards.

For example, take a look back at Figure 3.9 and notice in the left side of the screen that the American Express credit card has been selected. (It will be highlighted in green.) Above that are other options, including the All Accounts section, which provides a list that blends checking accounts, savings accounts, and investment accounts with any credit card accounts. It is a lot of information to sift through, but you can do it by clicking the All Accounts option.

Figure 3.20 shows how easy it is to jump from account to account. Clicking the United Bank option allows me to view a listing of all my checking account details. As with the credit card details, I can sort them, add tags, type in notes, and even export the data to a CSV file. All the features (and more) covered in this lesson for credit cards can be applied to checking accounts, savings accounts, and investment accounts.

Click to view other accounts

FIGURE 3.20   Jump from account to account with a single click.

Using Tags

Before we leave this lesson, let me show you how you can use tags after you link all your accounts (such as checking, savings, mortgage, automobile loan, and more).

After you assign tags to various credit card and checking account transactions, click on the Transactions tab shown in Figure 3.21.

FIGURE 3.21   Click the Transactions tab to use the Tag feature.

Scroll down and take a look at the existing tags (including any custom tags that you create—I made one called Reimbursable.) Figure 3.22 shows the tags list.

FIGURE 3.22   View your tags including custom tags created.

After clicking on the Reimbursable tab, Mint.com displays all checking account transactions as well as those made using a credit card that are tagged with the Reimbursable tag, as shown in Figure 3.23.

Showing 4 transactions	tagged as Reimbursable	or clear this search
☑ Edit Multiple		✛ Add a Transaction

	Date ▼	Description	Category	Amount
☐	MAY 13	Costco Gas	Gas & Fuel ▼	–$
☐	MAY 13	Ace Hardware EDIT DETAILS	Home Improvement	–$
☐	MAY 11	Home Depot	Home Improvement	–$
☐	APR 11	QuikTrip	Gas & Fuel	–$

FIGURE 3.23   View items that are grouped by a shared tag.

As you can see, you benefit when you tag your transactions by making it possible to view transactions stored in different types of accounts (mainly checking and credit card). I sometimes purchase items for my business using my personal debit card or credit card. These purchases need to be reimbursed for tax purposes, so I flag those items using the Reimbursable tag and then later write one check (from my business checking account) to cover them all. This is just one example of using tags. You might use tags for donations for end-of-year tax preparation, gasoline fill-ups for your company car, and more.

Summary

In this lesson, you learned how to link up a credit card to your Mint.com account and how to view credit card account information. You also learned to use tags, modify categories, and export your data to a CSV file. Finally, you also learned that you can perform all the same views and modifications available for a credit card account on your other account types.

Summary

LESSON 4

Loans

In this lesson, you learn how to link your various loans, such as a student loan or a mortgage, to Mint.com.

Your Loans

Mint.com is a great resource for tracking student loans, car loans, and even a mortgage. Mint.com gives you the capability to log in to one location and immediately view the details on all your loans, including information such as loan rates and principle amounts.

I hope you're beginning to see just how powerful Mint.com is when it comes to viewing your overall financial status. Instead of having to log in (and log out) of one website for every account you want to manage (checking, savings, credit cards, investments, and so on), you log in to Mint.com and get an immediate summary of your financial life.

Many people use Mint.com to track only their checking and savings accounts, preferring not to link up any debts (like credit cards and loans) that will appear front and center on the Overview page. But by not linking debt to their Mint.com account, they miss out on many other features (such as budgeting, planning, and alerts) that Mint.com makes available to users when they have all their financial data linked and up-to-date.

You've already seen how to link up credit card information to Mint.com and how easy it is to view the details of payments and charges made to those types of accounts. But credit cards are only one type of debt that Mint.com can monitor.

As you can see in Figure 4.1, Mint.com has no current information visible under the Loan category on the Overview page, but that's about to change.

FIGURE 4.1   Mint.com's Overview page shows an empty Loan category.

Now it's time to see how to link up two additional types of debt to your Mint.com account. The first is a standard loan and the second is a home mortgage.

Linking a Loan to Mint.com

Again, you can use two methods for linking loans to Mint.com. The first is to click the Add It Now! link shown in Figure 4.1. The second is to click the Your Accounts link in the upper-right corner of the screen. Both methods take you to the now-familiar screen shown in Figure 4.2.

Start by typing the name of the financial institution that maintains the loan. This could be a bank, a mortgage company, or other type of business.

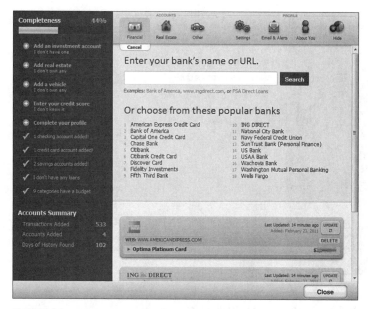

FIGURE 4.2   Finding your loan to link to Mint.com.

In Figure 4.3, I'm searching for Gulf Winds Federal Credit Union, where I financed my vehicle.

Mint.com may provide you with only one possible match, as shown in Figure 4.4, or you may get a longer list. Find the one that matches up to the type of loan you want to link to Mint.com and click that link. (Remember, even if you select the wrong financial institution, you won't be able to provide the correct user ID and password. So don't worry about adding someone else's loan to your Mint.com account.)

Figure 4.5 shows that I'm now asked to provide my Member Number and Password.

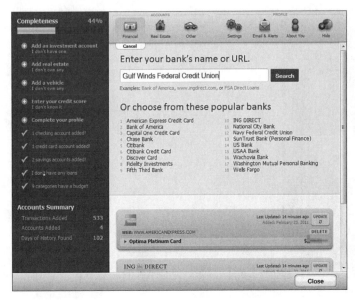

FIGURE 4.3　Searching for a credit union.

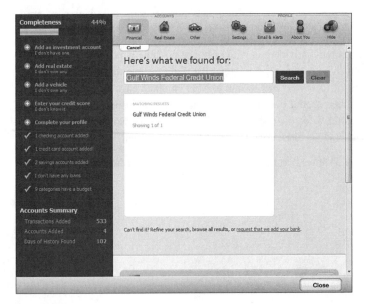

FIGURE 4.4　Click the link that matches up to your loan.

> TIP: **Requested Credentials May Have Different Titles**
>
> Some banks refer to your login name as User ID, but other options include Account Number, Member Name, Member ID, and many other variations. Mint.com will typically request the information using the same word(s) that a particular financial institution uses, so don't worry if the screen you see isn't an exact match to the ones shown here.

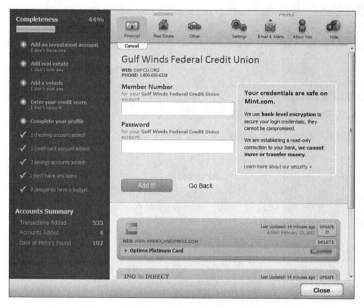

FIGURE 4.5   Provide login credentials requested to make the link.

After the link is made, the loan will be listed with your other accounts, as shown in Figure 4.6.

Notice that the vehicle loan amount (blurred) shown in Figure 4.7 is not negative. You will see debts shown as negative values only on the Overview page.

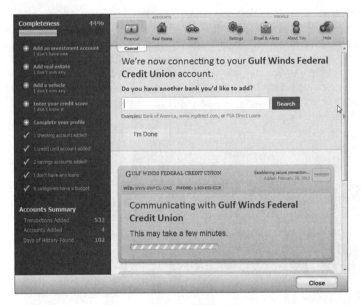

FIGURE 4.6   A loan is now being linked to Mint.com.

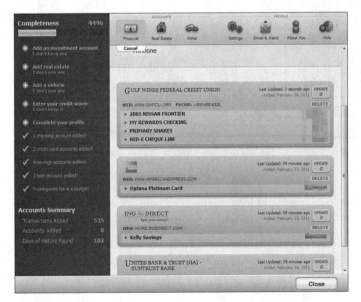

FIGURE 4.7   The total amount of a loan (blurred) is displayed.

Work through the linking procedure again to add a student loan or other personal loan. As Mint.com creates the link, the Loan category will continue to update and show you the balances on your loan debts.

Add a Mortgage

If you have a home or other property and have a mortgage, Mint.com is just as capable of linking to this loan information as your other types of accounts.

A mortgage is treated by Mint.com as a loan, so if this is the only type of loan you have, you can click the Add It Now! link under the Loan category (refer to Figure 4.1) or select Your Accounts and perform a search for your mortgage holder, as shown in Figure 4.8.

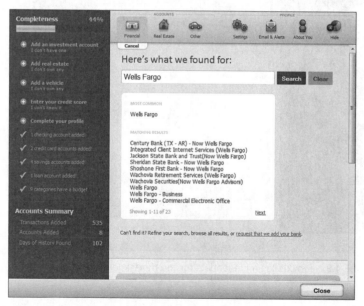

FIGURE 4.8 Search for your mortgage holder's name.

Sort through the list provided and select the best fit. In Figure 4.8, Wells Fargo was identified as the most common name, but look at the list of other organizations that also came up; most are affiliated with Wells Fargo, but be aware that in some instances the most common listing may not be the right one.

In this example, a user ID and password may be associated with an organization that is backed by Wells Fargo but has a unique name (such as Shoshone First Bank, which was purchased by Wells Fargo).

After clicking the correct link, you are again asked to provide login credentials, as shown in Figure 4.9. Notice that this time I am asked to provide either my Username or SSN (Social Security Number) along with a password.

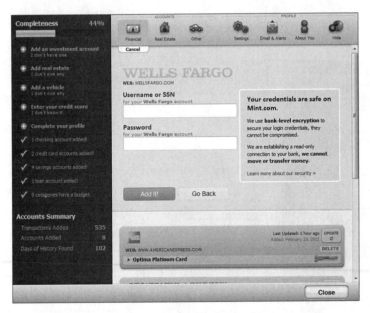

FIGURE 4.9　Provide login credentials for the mortgage account.

The linking process begins as shown in Figure 4.10.

After the mortgage account is linked, you can see the balance of the mortgage displayed along with your other account balances. Note that the value shown in Figure 4.11 (blurred in the figure) is a positive value, not negative. Mint.com will change this value to a negative value later on the Overview page. When Mint.com shows you the details of a linked account, the amount is always positive. But when Mint.com provides you an overall summary of your finances (on the Overview page) that includes your overall Net Worth, it displays debt as negative values so it's easier to distinguish income (and other positive cash flow) from debts.

FIGURE 4.10 Linking a mortgage to Mint.com.

For a new 30-year mortgage, don't be shocked when you see the value listed. Most homeowners cut a check each month for their mortgage and rarely take note of the balance change, knowing that the balance is quite large.

But don't let that value stop you from linking your mortgage information to Mint.com. One benefit of linking your debts (credit cards, loans, mortgage, and so on) to Mint.com is that Mint.com searches for better deals for

you—better interest rates, better monthly fees, and so on. Finding better
deals will be covered later in Lesson 10, "Ways to Save and Trends."

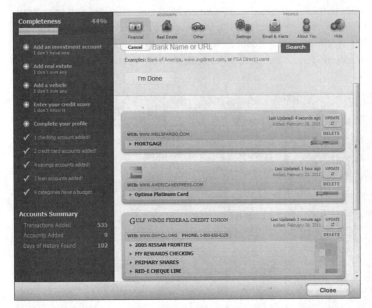

FIGURE 4.11   Your mortgage linked to Mint.com.

When you click the Close button, you return to the Overview page where
you can see that the Loan category is updated to show any loans that are
linked. Figure 4.12 shows both my mortgage and my vehicle loan.

Now that you understand how to link loans to Mint.com, you also need to
know how to view details of the loan. It's similar to what you learned in
Lesson 3, "Credit Cards," for viewing details of your credit cards, but in
this instance you need to provide some information that most loan
accounts don't provide to Mint.com.

FIGURE 4.12   Loan details on the Overview page.

Adding Loan Details

Under the Loan category on the Overview page, move your mouse pointer over the name of a loan until it becomes underlined, as shown in Figure 4.13. When the account is underlined, click your left mouse button to select it.

Clicking an account opens the window, shown in Figure 4.14, that lists all your accounts.

When you view your accounts in the Your Accounts window shown in Figure 4.14, you can move your mouse pointer over an account to see the Edit Details option appear, as shown in Figure 4.15.

Underlined
loan

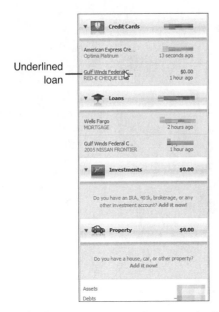

FIGURE 4.13 Summary of loans on the Overview page.

Click the account when Edit Details is visible, and a drop-down box appears. This drop-down box is slightly different for different types of accounts. For example, checking accounts won't have an APR box if they're not interest-bearing accounts.

For Figure 4.16, my vehicle loan is selected. You can see that Mint.com is asking me for some details about the loan that was not provided by Gulf Winds Federal Credit Union.

You do not have to provide this information to Mint.com. However, if provided, this level of information is used by Mint.com to search for financial organizations that can provide better deals (typically a better APR).

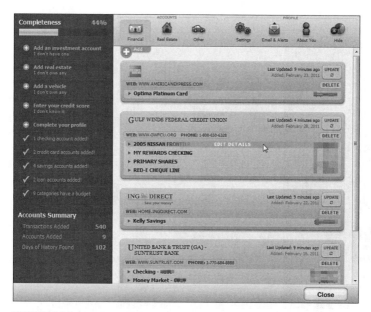

FIGURE 4.14 Your accounts can be clicked to edit or view details.

You can provide the interest rate on the loan as well as change the type of loan (such as Fixed or Variable). Again, this level of information isn't required by Mint.com, but taking the time to find this information and update the loan account can help you later if you're ever shopping for a new loan, refinancing, or just need to know this information quickly.

Figure 4.17 shows the same drop-down box for my mortgage. Again, I don't have to provide this information, but Mint.com can use it to search for better rates down the road.

The Edit Details option

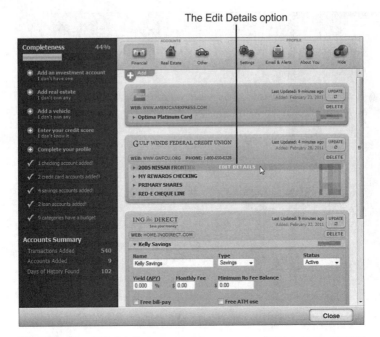

FIGURE 4.15   Edit details by moving the mouse pointer over an account.

Mint.com Progress Bar

Take a look at Figure 4.18 and you see that I've completed 44% of the Mint.com account creation process. I still need to add a few things, such as my investments, the value of my home, and possibly update Mint.com with my credit scores.

The progress bar is a useful feature for knowing how far along in the process you are, but keep in mind that you don't have to provide all information or link every account you have. Certainly it's beneficial to have as much of your financial information available to Mint.com as possible. This allows you to get an instant "picture" of your financial life, but it's not required.

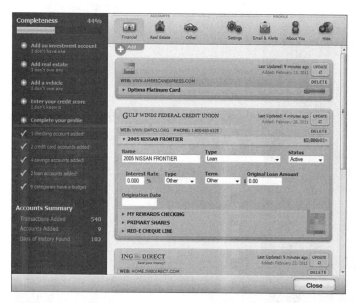

FIGURE 4.16 Mint.com requests details on some loans.

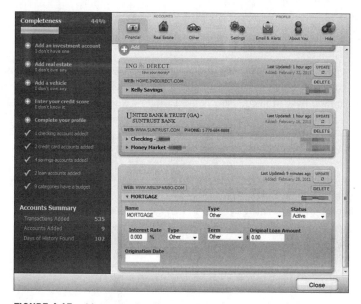

FIGURE 4.17 Mortgage details that Mint.com does not gather from my bank.

Percentage complete

FIGURE 4.18 Mint.com tracks account linking to calculate a percentage complete.

For example, I have no desire for Mint.com to store my credit report scores. Underneath that option, as shown in Figure 4.18, if I click the I Don't Know It link, Mint.com shows me a window where I can sign up with one of two services to obtain it, as shown in Figure 4.19. (I can also choose to rate my credit score (A, B, C, D, or F) instead of providing a value.)

Likewise, another option shown in Figure 4.18 allows me to enter a vehicle and its value if the loan is paid off. Otherwise, it goes under loans. I don't have a paid-off vehicle (yet) so I click the I Don't Own Any link and this option disappears, as shown in Figure 4.20. Notice also that my Mint.com percentage bar jumped from 44% to 50%.

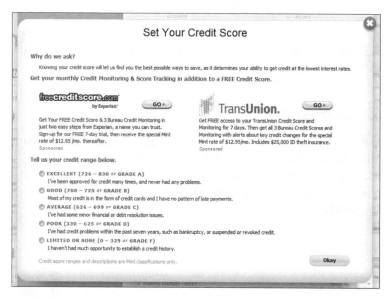

FIGURE 4.19 Update your credit scores if you want.

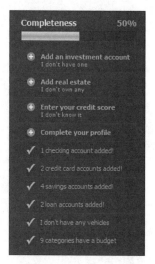

FIGURE 4.20 Jump from account to account with a single click.

As you update your Mint.com account, the percentage bar will move closer to 100%. But don't fret if it never hits 100%, because there may be some financial information that you don't want to share such as your credit score.

Summary

In this lesson, you learned how to link both a loan and a mortgage to your Mint.com account. You were also shown how to provide more details about the loan that aren't passed down by financial institutions. Finally, you learned how completing tasks in Mint.com increases the percentage complete bar.

LESSON 5

Investments and Account Updates

In this lesson, you learn how to link investments such as IRA and 401(k) accounts, stocks and bonds trading, and similar accounts. You also are shown how to identify an account that needs updating and the steps required to update it.

Your Investments

Mint.com can easily keep track of your checking and savings accounts, your credit cards, and your loans, so it should come as no surprise that Mint.com will also assist you when it comes to monitoring your investments.

People invest their money in a variety of ways; stocks, bonds, mutual funds, and commodities are just a few. Some of these investments are for retirement, such as IRA and 401(k) accounts, or possibly college/university funds such as 529 plans. Other investors put their money directly into specific stocks (such as Microsoft, Apple, or Coca-Cola) that have frequent fluctuations in their value, and still others invest in the traditionally safer and more stable bonds.

Whatever type of investing you do, it likely is done through an investment firm or other financial organization that provides you with monthly statements on the value(s) of your investments. Mint.com communicates with these financial organizations just as it does with credit cards, banking accounts, and other types of financial accounts.

If you don't have any investments or you haven't yet linked an investment to Mint.com, you see the Investments category on the Overview page listing a $0.00 amount, as shown in Figure 5.1.

FIGURE 5.1   Mint.com's Overview page shows the Investments category.

If you've been linking your accounts to Mint.com as you've read through the previous lessons, you already know how easy it's going to be to link an investment. We walk through that next.

Linking an Investment to Mint.com

For investments, there are two methods to link an account. The first is to click the Add It Now! link, shown in Figure 5.1, and the other is to click Your Accounts in the upper-right corner of the screen. Either method takes you to the account search screen shown in Figure 5.2.

Click the Add an Investment Account link in the left column, as shown in Figure 5.2. You see that investment accounts still require a search for the financial institution that manages the account for you. I enter **Oppenheimer Funds** into the search box.

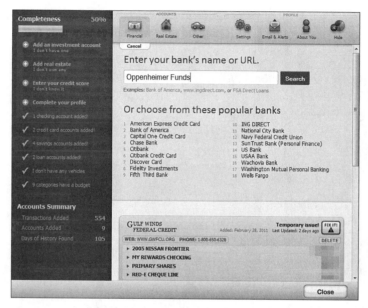

FIGURE 5.2   Finding investments to link to Mint.com.

Luckily, Oppenheimer Funds has a fairly unique name, and as you can see in Figure 5.3, it's the only option found. You might be presented with a list of possible organizations, depending on the name, so click the one that best matches your investment account's organization.

Again you are asked to provide a user ID and password to link to your investment account. Enter this information and click the Add It! button, as shown in Figure 5.4.

Communication between Mint.com and your investment account begins as shown in Figure 5.5. This could take a few seconds or a few minutes, depending on the organization and how much information must be exchanged between Mint.com and your account.

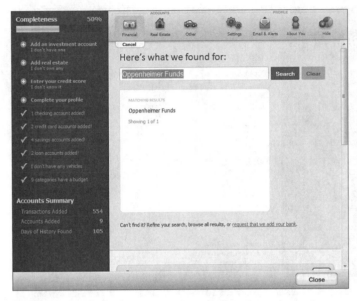

FIGURE 5.3 Find the best match from the list of search results.

FIGURE 5.4 Provide your login credentials to link the investment.

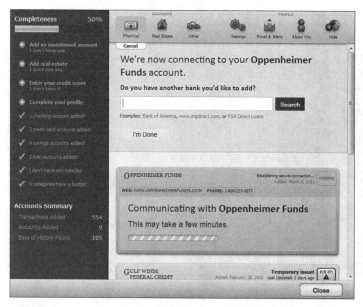

FIGURE 5.5   Mint.com will download financial information if the link is made.

If the link is successful, you now see the investment(s) from that account listed with your other accounts, as shown in Figure 5.6.

TIP: **More Than One Value for an Account**

If you see more than one value listed under an investment account you created, don't be alarmed. Many investments, especially retirement accounts, are spread out over multiple investment platforms, such as stocks, bonds, and mutual funds. In Figure 5.6, for example, the Oppenheimer Solo 401(k) consists of three separate mutual funds.

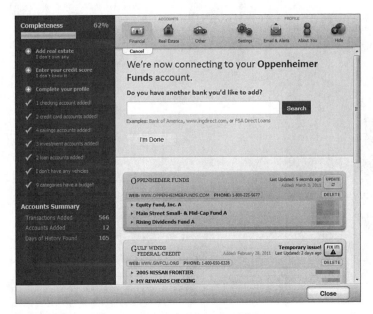

FIGURE 5.6   An investment account linked to Mint.com.

Update an Account

Your financial data needs to be protected. This is why Mint.com requires
you to not only provide your login credentials when you create a link, but
it also does not allow any kind of money transfer while logged in.
Mint.com's purpose is to allow you to view your financial data and have
access to tools to help increase your financial knowledge.

However, you may occasionally be asked by Mint.com to update an
account. There are multiple reasons for this: Accounts may require passwords to be changed periodically, Mint.com updates may force you to
resubmit login credentials, and more.

How do you know when an account needs to be updated? Take a look at
Figure 5.7; you may notice small yellow triangles with an exclamation
point inside. These small Update Alert icons may appear next to one or
more of your account types.

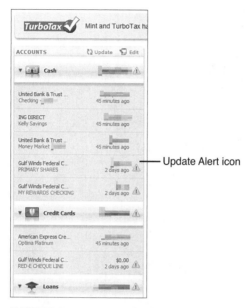

Update Alert icon

FIGURE 5.7 Update Alert icons let you know that something needs attention.

While an Update Alert icon is present, that account is not able to gather current financial information, and any values it currently displays may be out of date. This prevents Mint.com from providing you with an accurate Net Worth value and may also prevent a budget from updating (more on budgets in Lesson 8, "Budgets").

To update an account, click one of the Update Alert icons, as shown in Figure 5.8.

After clicking the Update Alert, any accounts that require your attention are displayed in a yellow box with a Fix It button, as shown in Figure 5.9.

Clicking the Fix It button can produce different results. You may be asked to provide a password if an account forces passwords to be changed periodically. Or it may reconnect to the account and ask you to provide some piece of information that is either missing or is required for a link to continue.

Click Update
Alert icon

FIGURE 5.8   Click an Update Alert icon to update an account.

After I click the Fix It button, I'm provided with a short description of the problem, as shown in Figure 5.10. In this instance, the connection was broken for an unknown reason, and Mint.com asks me to repair the link. (In this case, the Internet connection was severed during an update. I click the Try Again button after the Internet connection reestablishes.)

If the problem cannot be resolved, you can always delete the link and re-create it by clicking the Delete option shown in Figure 5.10. Re-create a link by searching for the organization, providing credentials, and relinking the account to your Mint.com account, as shown in Figure 5.11.

If you find you still cannot resolve the issue, you may need to call the financial organization to determine the problem. In this instance, a quick call to the credit union saved me a lot of frustration. As it turns out, the credit union had scheduled some maintenance on the online banking website, which made the site unavailable for three to four days. Figure 5.12 shows that the final error message I received indicates a failure to connect.

Fix It button

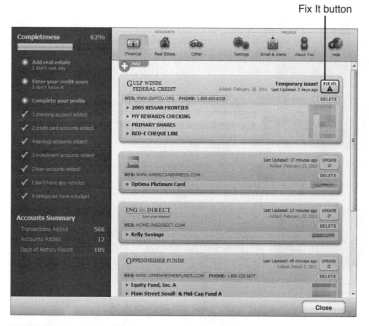

FIGURE 5.9   The Fix It button lets you know which account needs attention.

FIGURE 5.10   Get details on the problem by clicking Fix It.

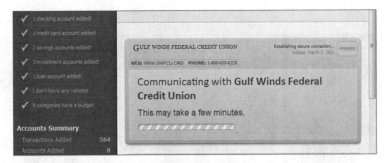

FIGURE 5.11   Deleting a link and re-creating it can fix some problems.

FIGURE 5.12   Failure to connect with an online site results in an error message.

If you should decide to remove an account, click the Delete button (see Figure 5.12) in the yellow box surrounding the account. You then see a window like the one in Figure 5.13. Type **Delete** into the text box, click Okay, and then re-create the link to see whether that resolves the problem.

Other Types of Investments

Before we leave this lesson, I want to make you aware of a special feature in Mint.com that allows you to enter in other types of investments that may not fall under the traditional definition (stocks, bonds, real estate).

Other types of investments include pieces of art, rare book collections, antiques, and more. Because these types of investments are often difficult to put a value on, Mint.com allows you to enter in the estimated value. This value remains constant, so you will have to manually update it if you find the value increasing or decreasing.

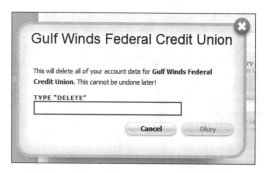

FIGURE 5.13 Deleting a link and re-creating it can fix a bad link.

If you want to enter in an investment of this type, start by clicking the Your Accounts link at the top-right corner of the screen, and then click the Other tab, shown in Figure 5.14.

Other tab

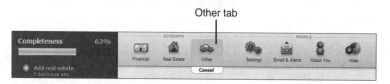

FIGURE 5.14 Other investments can be linked to Mint.com.

The Other tab offers you the capability to enter in not only other types of property, such as the value of an art collection, but it also allows you to provide a cash value. Maybe you have some money hidden away in your home as an emergency fund, for instance, or you might have a debt value, such as a personal non-interest loan from a family member.

You can also enter the value of a paid-in-full vehicle, whether it's a classic/antique car or just a daily-driver that you no longer owe money on but intend to keep. Select the Money (or Debt), Vehicle, or Other Property option shown in Figure 5.15 and click the Next button. Make certain to select a description from the drop-down menu that appears next to the selected option.

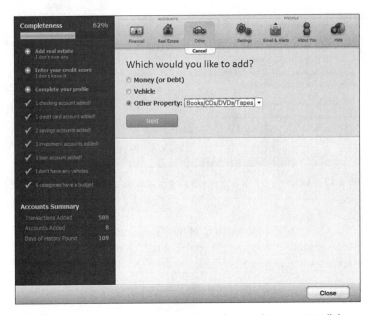

FIGURE 5.15   Select one of three options for creating a custom link.

The screen that appears next allows you to enter more details. For example, you can provide a more detailed name than the drop-down menu provided. Figure 5.16 is where I will enter **Rare Books** in the first text field and a value in the second field. (If this option is somehow related to another loan or investment, you can link this new amount to an existing one, and they are displayed in the same account information window.)

After adding a name and value, click the Add It! button and your new link is listed under the Other tab, as shown in Figure 5.17.

If you decide you want to update a value (increasing or decreasing it), you need to manually edit the new link you created. Move your mouse pointer over the new item until you see the Edit Details link appear, as shown in Figure 5.18.

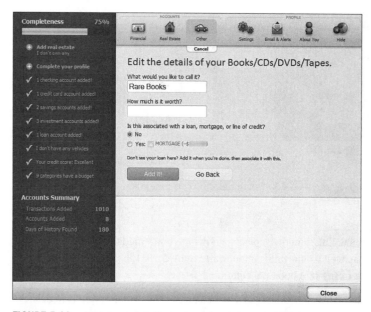

FIGURE 5.16   Add more details and a value to your new link.

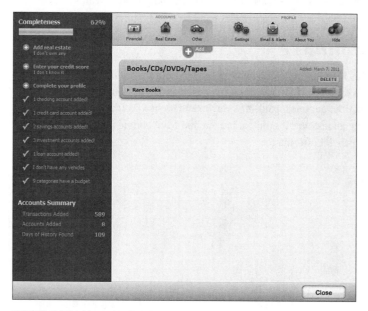

FIGURE 5.17   Your new link is created under the Other tab.

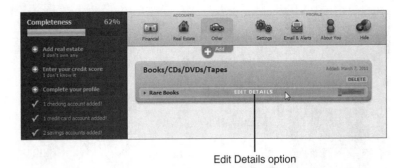

Edit Details option

FIGURE 5.18   Use Edit Details to modify a new link.

The new link window expands, allowing you to modify the name of the link as well as the value amount. In Figure 5.19, I increased the estimated value of my rare book collection.

Click the Close button to save the changes. Your other option is to delete the new link by clicking the Delete button (see Figure 5.19) which I just did, because my rare book collection exists only in my dreams.

Summary

In this lesson, you learned how to link to both traditional investments (stocks, bonds, IRA, and so on) as well as nontraditional investments (art collection, antiques, paid-off vehicle, and so on). You also learned how to update an account if a link is broken and Mint.com is not able to update the financial information.

Delete button

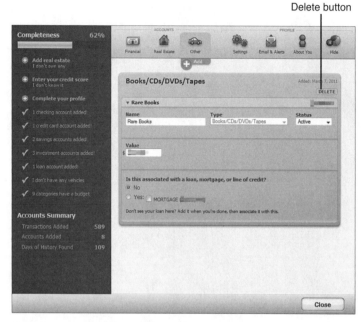

FIGURE 5.19   Update the name or value of a link.

LESSON 6

Email and SMS Alerts

In this lesson, you learn how Mint.com keeps you informed about your linked accounts using email and text messaging. You also learn how to configure alerts to trigger a notice when certain transactions or events occur and how to refine your alerts by turning on and off those that are useful to you.

Stay Alert

Mint.com does such a good job of summarizing your overall "financial health" on the Overview page that you may sometimes forget to dive down into the details of individual accounts and examine your data for unusual activity. It can become too easy to just view your current cash balance and credit card debt totals and forget to poke around in the actual transactions.

Fortunately, Mint.com is a vigilant tool, and it looks for transactions in your accounts that don't fit with your normal routine. It's also constantly looking at your expenditures and comparing them to any budget you may have created. (You learn about Budgets next in Lesson 8, "Budgets.") But for Mint.com to maintain a careful watch over your financial life, you must first instruct Mint.com on how you want it to perform these duties and when to alert you.

Mint.com has some limited watchdog features already turned on, and these are typically found on the Overview page as shown in Figure 6.1.

These built-in alerts mainly pertain to your spending habits, and Mint.com will let you know when a transaction (or number of transactions) exceeds previous monthly spending habits. It's a start, but Mint.com is capable of much higher levels of monitoring, as outlined in this lesson.

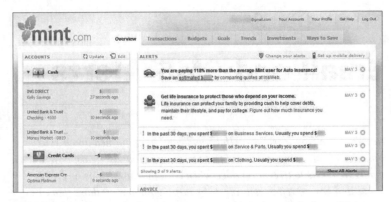

FIGURE 6.1   Mint.com's Overview page contains a few alerts from Mint.com

Basic Alerts

Mint.com's Overview page has a section devoted entirely to alerts. You are typically shown the first three alerts (see Figure 6.1), but you must click the Show All Alerts button indicated in Figure 6.2 to get the full listing.

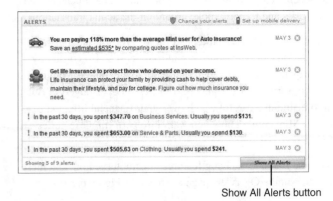

Show All Alerts button

FIGURE 6.2   Only a few alerts are visible at first.

After clicking the Show All Alerts button, the list expands to show much more.

Figure 6.3 shows how Mint.com organizes your alerts as well, with icons that represent items such as fees or deposits.

FIGURE 6.3 More alerts are visible with icons to help identify alert types.

An exclamation point icon is typically used to represent a budget-related item, a dollar sign represents a deposit, and the Fee icon represents, surprise, a fee that's been assessed on an account (such as a monthly fee for checking or an interest charge).

Other icons represent special deals that Mint.com may be offering—these include chances to reduce credit card interest rates, refinancing opportunities for automobiles and homes, and more. Clicking a link associated with these types of alerts like the ones in Figure 6.4 opens a new window where you can read information about how to take advantage of a money-saving feature.

You can remove an alert from the list by clicking the small X to the right of the alert, as shown in Figure 6.5.

If you remove all the alerts, you see a message like the one shown in Figure 6.6.

Click for more details

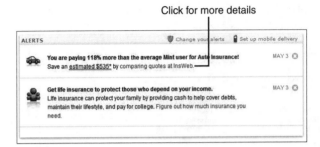

FIGURE 6.4   Special money-saving opportunities are also displayed as alerts.

Click to remove alert

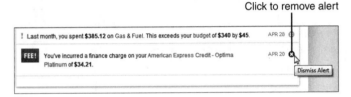

FIGURE 6.5   Remove an alert after you review it.

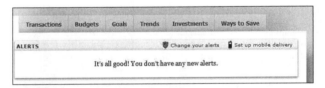

FIGURE 6.6   Clearing your alerts is a good habit to develop.

TIP: **Alerts Aren't All Bad**

Although most of Mint.com's alerts are related to unusually high charges or service fees, it's apparent over time that many of the alerts can be extremely useful, especially if you set up your account to send them via email (covered later in this lesson) or mobile phone (covered in Lesson 11, "Mint.com Mobile Versions"). If you know how much a credit card is charging you per month for service fees, it can help you make decisions later when it comes to finding a better deal.

If you find that the number of alerts is too large, or if you prefer not to receive an alert about particular accounts, you need to spend some time tweaking the Mint.com settings, including specifying an email address (if you want alerts emailed to you) and setting threshold values for various alerts to trigger.

Configuring Alerts

There are two main methods for accessing the Alert settings in Mint.com. The first is to click the Change Your Alerts link shown in Figure 6.7.

Click to configure alerts

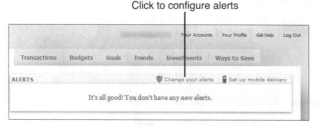

FIGURE 6.7   Configure alerts using the Change Your Alerts link.

The second way to access the Alert settings is to click Your Accounts in the upper-right corner of the Overview page and then click the Email & Alerts tab, as shown in Figure 6.8. (If you click the Change Your Alerts link in Figure 6.7, you go directly to this screen.)

The first thing you can do on this page is to decide whether you even want to receive email alerts. The default setting is for a Weekly summary to be emailed to the primary email address associated with your Mint.com account.

Click the drop-down menu shown in Figure 6.9 and choose a Weekly or Monthly summary, or select Never to turn this feature off completely.

You can also click the Add One link to add a secondary email address for alerts; this is useful for a spouse, for example, to also get a weekly or monthly summary report.

FIGURE 6.8 The Email & Alerts screen is for configuring alerts.

Lesson 11 explains how to access Mint.com via your mobile phone, but in Figure 6.10 you see that if you provide your mobile phone number, you can also receive a weekly summary via text messaging (monthly is not an option).

TIP: **Text Messaging Fees**

Although Mint.com sends no more than 10 alert messages per month, be aware that the weekly summary sent to a mobile phone may be so long that it is divided over multiple text messages. This may not be an issue for you if you have unlimited text messaging with your carrier, but if you don't have unlimited text messaging, remember to set the delivery option to Never if you find that the number of text messages received from Mint.com is large.

Select delivery period

FIGURE 6.9   Choose whether to receive email summaries and when.

After you enter your mobile number, click the Send button; a confirmation code is sent (via text message on your mobile phone) that you need to enter in the Confirm Your Activation Code text box. Click the Finish button as shown in Figure 6.11. After you provide the activation code, you are able to receive text message summaries from Mint.com.

TIP: **Disabling Mobile Phone Alerts**

You can easily disable text messages from Mint.com at any time by clicking the Deactivate button that appears to the right of your phone number on the Email & Alerts tab. Or reply to a text message with only the word "STOP" in the message.

FIGURE 6.10 Receive alerts via text messaging.

FIGURE 6.11 Your mobile phone must be activated to receive email summaries from Mint.com.

Now scroll down the Email & Alerts page a bit to find even more configurable alert settings, as shown in Figure 6.12.

FIGURE 6.12 Find specific alerts of interest to you and turn them on or off.

The first thing to note is that there are two columns of check boxes—one for receiving alerts via email and the other for receiving alerts via SMS (text messaging). A check in a box under the SMS column but an empty box under the Email column means that you will receive an alert only for that specific alert type via text messaging.

Figure 6.13 shows that all text message alerts except for low balance are turned off. (The amount to trigger an alert can be selected from the dropdown menu and includes $0, $50, $100, $200, $500, $1,000, and $2,000.)

Figure 6.13 also shows that I elect to receive an email alert (weekly) that contains information where transactions exceed $200.00 on average. I have quite a few legitimate payments and charges that exceed that level, so I

FIGURE 6.13   Configuring both email and text messaging alerts is simple.

could easily bump it up to $500 or more, but I still want to know when Mint.com identifies transactions for $200 or more. Feel free to adjust this based on your comfort and spending levels.

Scroll down the Email & Alerts tab a bit more and you see the remaining alerts that can be configured, as shown in Figure 6.14.

As you can see in Figure 6.15, I'm not very fond of bank fees, so the minimum amount is set to $1 to let me know if my banks tries anything sneaky. I also set the minimum threshold for a single purchase to $1,000.00; if Mint.com sees any single purchase over that amount, I get an immediate text message.

If you don't want to receive alerts related to ways you can save money (on credit card interest rates, for example), Figure 6.16 shows the four boxes that can be unchecked so you won't receive these special messages.

FIGURE 6.14 More alerts are available on the Email & Alerts tab.

FIGURE 6.15 Bank fees and large purchases can be flagged.

FIGURE 6.16   Turn off special deals by unchecking these four boxes.

Finally, scroll down just a bit more and you see the final three alerts that can be configured, as shown in Figure 6.17.

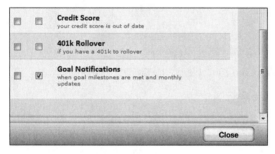

FIGURE 6.17   The final alerts that Mint.com can email or text you regarding.

If you choose to let Mint.com access your credit score, you can also choose to be told when it's out of date. Additional alerts include the option of being notified whether a 401k can be rolled over and when a goal is met. (Goals are covered in Lesson 8.) I turned off the first two options, but leave them checked if they are relevant to you and your needs.

After turning on or off alerts, click the Close button and you're done! You begin to receive weekly or monthly email messages from Mint.com that display the same information as shown on the Overview page, plus alerts related to any you configured on the Email & Alerts tab.

You also begin to receive customized alerts (via email and/or text messaging) for those thresholds that you set such as for large purchases.

You can always refine your alerts by accessing the Email & Alerts tab again to tweak, disable, or turn on existing or new alerts.

Summary

In this lesson, you learned how Mint.com can keep you informed about your financial information via text messages and emails. You learned how to customize these alerts so they are useful to you and your specific financial situation.

LESSON 7

Categories

In this lesson, you learn how to use the Category feature that Mint.com relies on for the proper functioning of its Budget and Goals tools. You learn how to view, change, and create categories that are assigned to transactions.

Creating a Budget or Setting Goals

After Mint.com is up and running, with all your accounts configured properly, you'll want to learn about two of Mint.com's most useful features—Budgets and Goals.

Budgets is much more than setting upper limits on different spending categories (food, gas, entertainment, and the like). It's a tool that allows users to identify spending habits, test out "what if" scenarios with potential purchases, and find ways to reduce their expenses by identifying where the money goes and where it might be better spent.

Goals is a nice feature that allows Mint.com users to set up special categories, such as a vacation or a special event (wedding, new car, and so on) and monitor how their savings and spending affect those end goals.

Before you begin using the Mint.com Budgets or Goals tools, log in to your Mint.com account. You see that the Budget feature is already running and available on the Overview page, as shown in Figure 7.1. The Goals category should be empty (also shown in Figure 7.1) unless you've already played around with that feature and set a goal or two of your own.

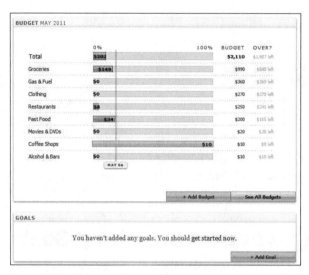

FIGURE 7.1 Mint.com's Overview page already has the Budget feature up and running.

Even though the budget feature is running, you may discover some errors if you look closely. For example, in Figure 7.1 you'll notice that I spent $0 in the Gas & Fuel category. This is inaccurate because I know that either my wife or I visit the gas station at least once a week, and sometimes both of us need a fill-up.

So what's the problem here? The problem is that Mint.com hasn't properly identified transactions that represent the purchase of gasoline for one or both of my family's vehicles. Before I can properly use the Budgets (and Goals) tool, I need to fix this issue.

Transaction Categories

The Budget tool built in to Mint.com is only as accurate and useful as you allow it to be. This means that for it to help you monitor your spending on shoes, for example, you must first help Mint.com to identify where shoes are typically purchased (such as a shoe store name), or you must go in and manually configure an expenditure (in your checking account, for example) as a shoe purchase.

Figure 7.2 shows a few transactions in my checking account. The first problem is that it shows a Disney purchase of $20.87 flagged as travel. That sort of makes sense because Disney is a popular tourist attraction, but in this instance it was a birthday present purchased from the Disney Store. Fortunately, fixing that error is simple.

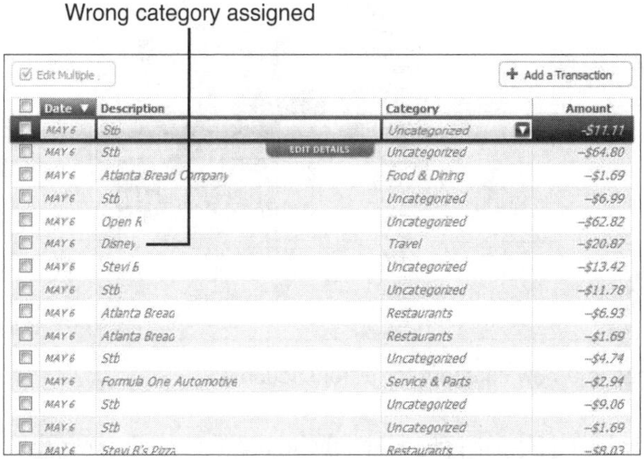

Wrong category assigned

FIGURE 7.2   Identify category errors for your purchase transactions.

I first click anywhere on the line that makes up an individual transaction. In Figure 7.3, I click the line containing the Disney transaction, and all of that line's categories (Date, Description, Category, and Amount) are selected.

FIGURE 7.3   Select a transaction to modify its data.

If I click the small triangle in the Category column, I get a list of all the various category names that Mint.com recognizes. Many of those categories have subcategories as well; be careful when selecting categories as the Category feature will be just as useless to you if you leave a transaction uncategorized as it will be if you miscategorize it.

In Figure 7.4, I select the Gifts & Donations category and then select the Gift subcategory.

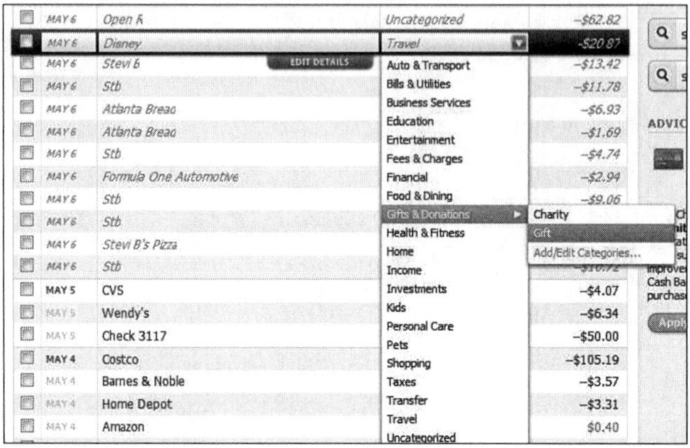

FIGURE 7.4   Choose a new category for a transaction.

My newly selected category is applied, and the transaction now shows the purchase is flagged as a Gift and not as Travel, as shown in Figure 7.5.

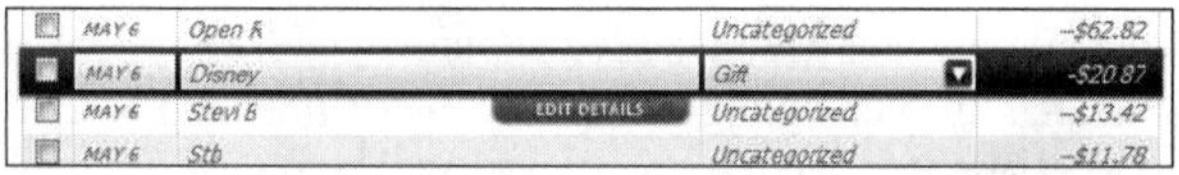

FIGURE 7.5   The transaction has the correct category assigned.

Assigning a Category to Multiple Transactions

Notice in Figure 7.6 that a handful of transactions are mislabeled as Restaurant for the Atlanta Bread Company. I can go down and assign each a category manually, just as I did in the previous example, but there's a faster way, especially if you have many transactions that use the same category.

	Date	Description	Category	Amount
☑ Edit Multiple				✚ Add a Transaction
■	MAY 6	Atlanta Bread	Restaurants ▼	–$1.69
☐	MAY 6	Atlanta Bread EDIT DETAILS	Restaurants	–$6.93
☐	MAY 6	Atlanta Bread Company	Coffee Shops	–$1.69
☐	MAY 6	Disney	Gift	–$20.87
☐	MAY 6	Formula One Automotive	Service & Parts	–$2.94
☐	MAY 6	Open K	Uncategorized	–$62.82
☐	MAY 6	Stb	Uncategorized	–$10.72
☐	MAY 6	Stb	Uncategorized	–$1.69
☐	MAY 6	Stb	Uncategorized	–$9.06
☐	MAY 6	Stb	Uncategorized	–$4.74
☐	MAY 6	Stb	Uncategorized	–$11.78
☐	MAY 6	Stb	Uncategorized	–$6.99
☐	MAY 6	Stb	Uncategorized	–$64.80
☐	MAY 6	Stb	Uncategorized	–$11.11
☐	MAY 6	Stevi b	Uncategorized	–$13.42
☐	MAY 6	Stevi B's Pizza	Restaurants	–$8.03

FIGURE 7.6   Identify transactions that share an identical category.

CAUTION: **Changing a Correct Transaction Category**

One other possibility when it comes to categories is that Mint.com may correctly categorize a transaction (such as indicating a charge as Book) but you may still want to change it to a more descriptive category such as Gift. You can only assign one category to a transaction, so pick the one that best fits the transaction but also best matches how you want to group that transaction among other charges.

TIP: **Changing a Transaction Category Is Universal**

If you have two or more transactions with the same business, changing one of the transaction categories will not automatically change the other. For example, changing a QT (Quick Trip) transaction to Fuel for that fill-up I had yesterday won't change the earlier QT transaction showing Fast Food (for that lunch-on-the-go hot dog) to Fuel.

All I have to do is place a check mark in the check box next to each transaction that I want to assign an identical category. Figure 7.7 shows that I selected three transactions with the same company.

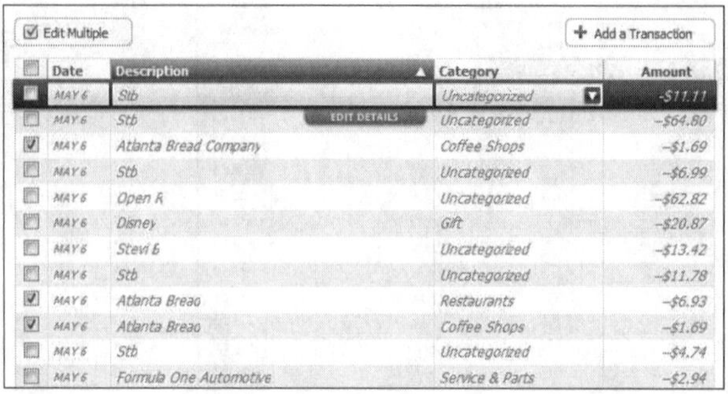

FIGURE 7.7   Check the boxes for transactions that share a common category.

Next, click the Edit Multiple button shown in Figure 7.8.

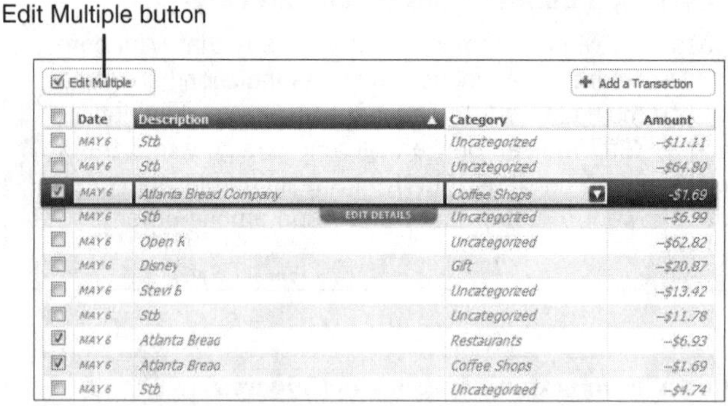

Edit Multiple button

FIGURE 7.8   Use the Edit Multiple button to make changes to two or more selected transactions.

A window opens like the one shown in Figure 7.9. You can apply a tag (or multiple tags) to all the selected transactions, modify the description name (I could change Atlanta Bread Company to ABC, for example), and add a note that is applied to all selected transactions.

Click the Category drop-down menu and assign all three transactions to the Coffee Shops category, as shown in Figure 7.10.

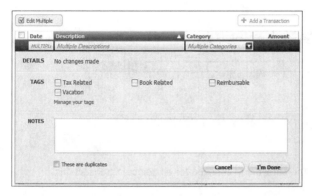

FIGURE 7.9   Modify multiple selected transactions at once.

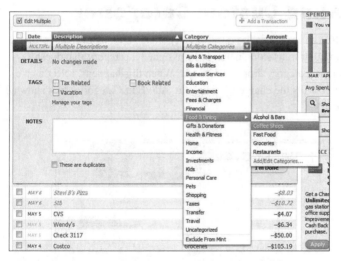

FIGURE 7.10   Select a category to apply to all selected transactions.

Click the I'm Done button (refer to Figure 7.9) to apply the changes to all the selected transactions. Compare Figure 7.11 to Figure 7.8 and you see that all three Atlanta Bread Company charges now have the Coffee Shop category assigned.

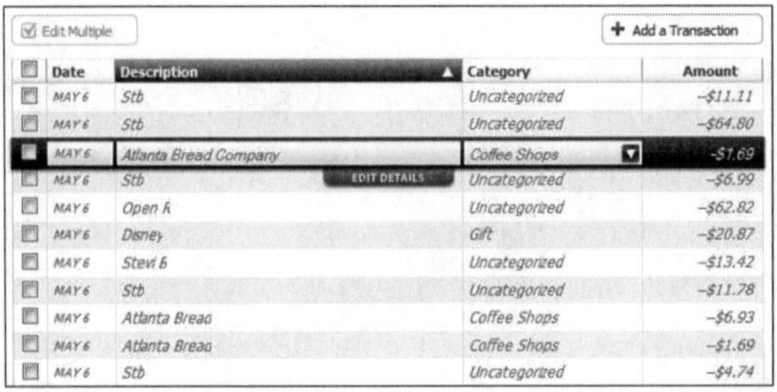

FIGURE 7.11   The category is changed for all selected transactions.

Creating Custom Categories

Although Mint.com has a long list of categories, you may eventually find that a particular transaction needs to be assigned a category that doesn't appear in the Category drop-down menu. When this happens, select a category that best fits the charge and click the Add/Edit Categories link shown in Figure 7.12.

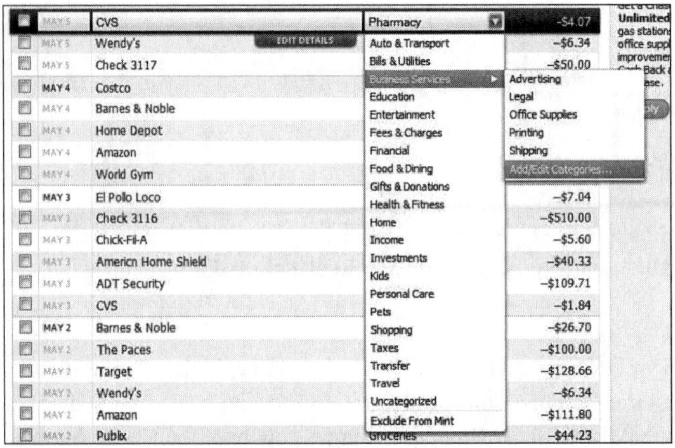

FIGURE 7.12   You can create your own category for a transaction.

I frequently make purchases for supplies needed for my books using my personal checking account, so I want to create a custom category so I can track these and reimburse myself from my company's checking account.

After selecting the Add/Edit Categories link, a window appears like the one in Figure 7.13.

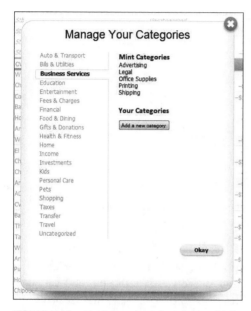

FIGURE 7.13 Custom categories are useful for assigning to special purchases.

Click the Add a New Category button (see Figure 7.13) and type in your new category name, as shown in Figure 7.14. Click the Save It button when you're done, and then click the OK button.

TIP: **Custom Subcategories**

Any new category you create is actually a subcategory of the larger list of categories that Mint.com provides. There does not currently appear to be a way to add a top-level category; therefore, you must select the best fit for your new custom category from the top-level list and then create your new category as a subcategory.

FIGURE 7.14   Add your custom category as a subcategory.

After creating a custom category, you can select a transaction (or multiple transactions) and see your custom category by selecting the top-level category you place it in. Figure 7.15 shows that my Book Reimbursements custom category is now a subcategory of the Business Services top-level category.

Credit Cards and Categories

The previous examples shown were all transactions from my personal checking account. But you can also assign categories to individual charges that are made and shown on any credit card account that is linked to Mint.com.

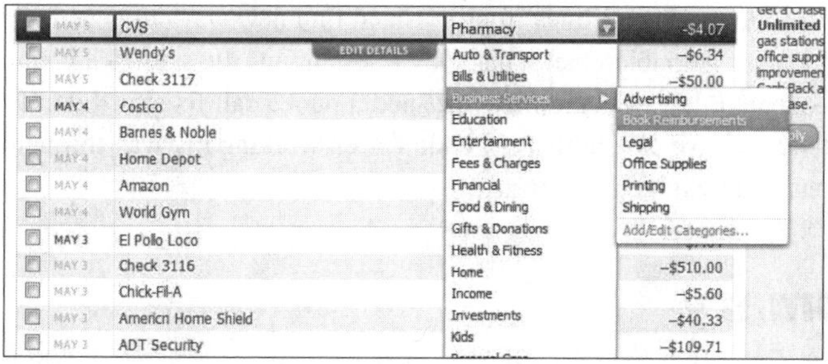
MAY 5 CVS Pharmacy -$4.07
MAY 5 Wendy's -$6.34
EDIT DETAILS
MAY 5 Check 3117 -$50.00
MAY 4 Costco
MAY 4 Barnes & Noble
MAY 4 Home Depot
MAY 4 Amazon
MAY 4 World Gym
MAY 3 El Pollo Loco
MAY 3 Check 3116 -$510.00
MAY 3 Chick-Fil-A -$5.60
MAY 3 Americn Home Shield -$40.33
MAY 3 ADT Security -$109.71
Auto & Transport
Bills & Utilities
Business Services
Education
Entertainment
Fees & Charges
Financial
Food & Dining
Gifts & Donations
Health & Fitness
Home
Income
Investments
Kids
Advertising
Book Reimbursements
Legal
Office Supplies
Printing
Shipping
Add/Edit Categories...
Unlimited
gas stations
office suppl
improvemen

FIGURE 7.15 Assign your new custom category to transactions.

Figure 7.16 shows that one of the charges on my American Express card has not been categorized. (And a few are incorrectly categorized—that March of Dimes is a donation, not a Health & Fitness!)

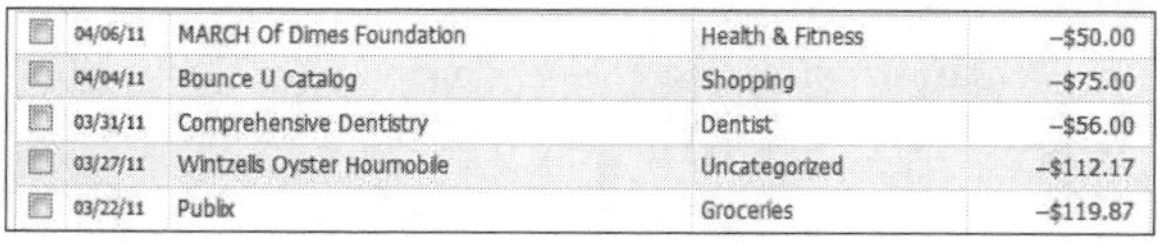

04/06/11	MARCH Of Dimes Foundation	Health & Fitness	-$50.00
04/04/11	Bounce U Catalog	Shopping	-$75.00
03/31/11	Comprehensive Dentistry	Dentist	-$56.00
03/27/11	Wintzells Oyster Houmobile	Uncategorized	-$112.17
03/22/11	Publix	Groceries	-$119.87

FIGURE 7.16 Categories are also found in credit card accounts.

If, later on, you choose to use either the Budgets or Goals tools, be certain that your checking account transactions and your credit card transactions are properly categorized. Typically, when you make a payment to your credit card company, a single charge shows up in your checking account. The only way you know how that amount is divided up among the various charges made to the card is to assign categories to each individual charge.

It's time consuming at first, but Mint.com begins to figure out your spending habits and gets better at assigning the correct categories. But it's not really a bad idea to go through your checking and credit card charges anyway—you might catch a fraudulent charge or an incorrect amount or "new" bank fees that are all the rage these days as the banking industry attempts to follow in the airlines' footsteps and find new ways to generate income. I caught a double-charge made by a restaurant (the same $ amount on two sequential days was the first clue) and a phone call fixed it. I don't know if I would have caught that if I hadn't been working my way through transactions and assigning categories.

Summary

In this lesson, you learned how Mint.com helps you to organize your expenditures using a set of categories. You learned how to assign categories to transactions, how to edit them, and how to create your own custom categories.

LESSON 8

Budgets

In this lesson, you learn how to use the Budgets tool to create, edit, and delete budget categories. You learn how using the Budgets tool helps you identify spending habits and how it alerts you when you go over a budget.

Budgeting Made Simple

Having your account transactions properly categorized (see Lesson 7, "Categories") is a major benefit when it's time to create a budget with Mint.com. For most people, budget seems to be a bad word, but many Mint.com users insist it's one of the best features of Mint.com because it allows you to better understand where your money is going month-to-month and year-to-year.

Mint.com allows you to create a personal budget to put into practice. You then use the Budgets tool to accurately track your spending and see where changes can or should be made. After your budget is up and running, you can try out various "what if" scenarios by changing values here and there to see short-term and long-term effects on your accounts and your goals (covered in Lesson 9, "Goals").

As you saw in Lesson 7, logging in to Mint.com provides you with a basic budget that has already been populated with your spending history. Figure 8.1 shows Mint.com's best guess as to what my budget values would be for categories such as groceries, clothes, fuel, and more.

Look closely at Figure 8.1 and you can see that Mint.com is telling me I've already reached my monthly coffee budget limit of $10 (and it's only May 10, 2011—I have 20 days left). It has also budgeted $990 for groceries; I don't know about you, but I rarely ever come close to spending $600 a month on groceries. So there's some obvious work for me to do here with the Budget tool.

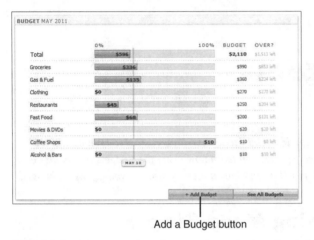

Add a Budget button

FIGURE 8.1   Mint.com's Overview page has a budget that is likely incorrect from the start.

Creating a New Budget

There are two ways to get started with creating a budget. The first is to click the Add Budget button shown in Figure 8.1. You can also click the Budgets tab on the Overview page that is shown in Figure 8.2.

Budgets tab

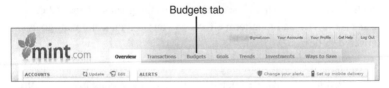

FIGURE 8.2   Select the Budgets tab to start building a budget.

Both methods will take you to the Budgets page shown in Figure 8.3. Notice that the information on this page may still contain irrelevant or incorrect budget values that are initially set by Mint.com. You can change those soon enough.

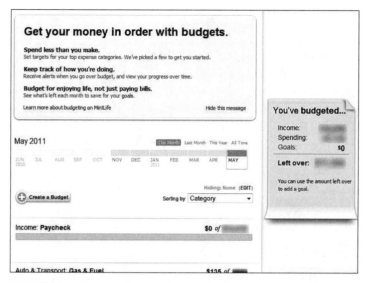

FIGURE 8.3 Start creating a budget on the Budgets page.

The first thing you should do is click the Create a Budget button shown in Figure 8.3. Clicking that button immediately opens a new window like the one shown in Figure 8.4.

Click the Choose a Category drop-down menu, and you see a long list of categories that can be monitored by the Budgets tool, as shown in Figure 8.5.

I want to set a budget (to monitor my spending) for books, which is found under the Shopping category, as shown in Figure 8.5. Notice also in Figure 8.5 that you can create custom categories. (You learned how to do this in Lesson 7.) I select Books as my category, as shown in Figure 8.6.

The first thing you notice after selecting a category is that Mint.com provides you with a bar graph that shows six months' worth of spending in that category, along with an average spending value. Figure 8.6 tells me I spent an average of $59 per month (from Dec 2010 to May 2011), and the graph tells me that February was my highest level of spending at close to $100.00.

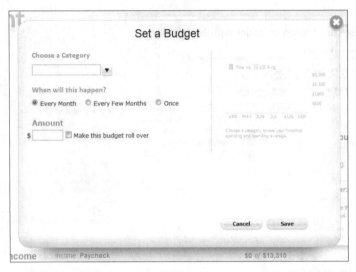

FIGURE 8.4   The Set a Budget window allows you to select categories and associated spending limits.

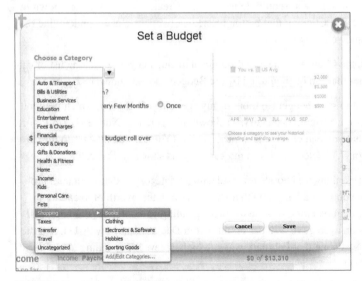

FIGURE 8.5   You can use the Budgets tool to monitor existing categories.

Books category

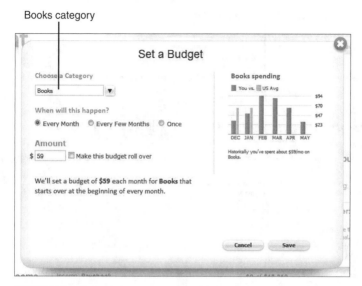

FIGURE 8.6 Selecting a category provides average spending habits.

TIP: **Averages Are Just Averages**

One high or low-spending month can easily affect the five months that are used to generate the average spending value. Keep this in mind as you try to set a realistic spending threshold for your budget categories. February is fairly typical of my spending habits per month, and January and December are my slowest book buying months as I attempt to recover from holiday spending. $75 or more is much more realistic—I'm a technical writer, so I buy a lot of books for research and self-training—so I'm going to ignore Mint.com's $59 suggested threshold and bump it up a bit.

Below the Choose a Category drop-down menu, you are asked to select a time period for this category. Your options include Every Month, Every Few Months (useful for quarterly automatic payments, for example), and Once, as shown in Figure 8.7.

Frequency of budget monitoring

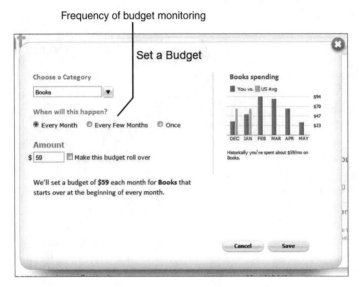

FIGURE 8.7   Select how often to monitor a budget category.

For some spending, you can be reasonably certain that an item will happen only once. For example, homeowners may have a once-a-year charge for membership dues in a homeowner's association. Or you may budget a flat amount of $500 per year for new tires for your car. Remember, just because you budget something doesn't mean you have to spend it. By adding your anticipated charges, Mint.com is better able to help you monitor your spending and balances and alert you when spending in one category puts your budgeted amount for other categories at risk.

For my Books category, I select the Every Month option—I'm a book fanatic and I can't remember the last time I didn't visit the bookstore at least once in a given week. When it comes to setting a budget, the best advice is to be true to yourself and then be honest with your budget settings. So, knowing that I spend a set amount each month, it's now time to figure out how much I want to budget for book expenditures.

Figure 8.8 shows that I entered a value of $100.00 for the Amount, and I placed a check in the check box for Make This Budget Roll Over, ensuring that my budget resets at the beginning of each month. This, in turn, gives me a better result in the averaging field later on should I revisit this budget category (more on this shortly).

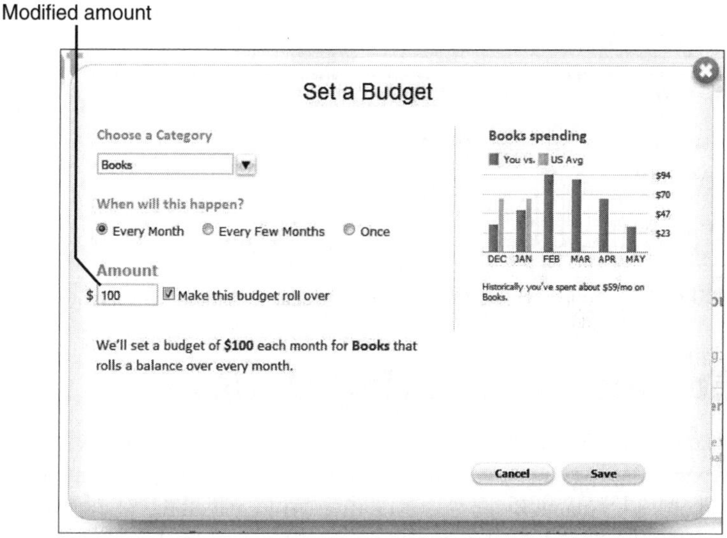

Modified amount

FIGURE 8.8   Provide a budget amount and decide if it resets each month.

Last, click the Save button (see Figure 8.8). Now scroll down the page a bit, and you find your new budget category and value added to the list of budget categories, as shown in Figure 8.9.

You now know how to add a budget category, but how do you handle those existing categories with (possibly) inaccurate amounts assigned to them? You need to edit or delete existing categories.

Auto & Transport: **Gas & Fuel**	$135 *of* $360
Entertainment: **Movies & DVDs**	$0 *of* $20
Food & Dining: **Alcohol & Bars**	$0 *of* $10
Food & Dining: **Coffee Shops**	$10 *of* $10
Food & Dining: **Fast Food**	$68 *of* $200
Food & Dining: **Groceries**	$336 *of* $990
Food & Dining: **Restaurants**	$45 *of* $250
Shopping: **Books**	$30 *of* $100
Shopping: **Clothing**	$0 *of* $270

FIGURE 8.9   Your new budget category is visible in the category list.

Editing an Existing Budget

Take a look at Figure 8.9 and you see that the Coffee Shops budget is still wrong. Mint.com set the maximum amount at $10.00. Given that my second office is Atlanta Bread Company (free Wi-Fi and all the $1.50 sweet tea I can drink) and that I do my best crunch-time writing here, that amount is simply too low.

To change an existing budget item, move your mouse pointer over the item to be changed and click the Edit Details button that appears, like the one shown in Figure 8.10.

Again I'm provided with a six-month bar graph along with an average spending value ($6.00 in this case). But I know that this is incorrect because the months of January and February have been averaged in, and these are my slowest work months. Given that I've already spent $10 and it's only May 10, 2011, it goes to reason that another 20 days will likely bump that spending up to around $30 or so. So I change the Once a Month value of $10.00 to $30.00, as shown in Figure 8.11. I make this reset each month by placing a check in the Make This Budget Roll Over check box and click the Save button.

Edit Details button

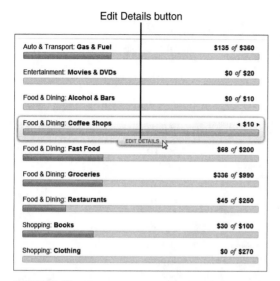

FIGURE 8.10   Editing a budget is a button click away.

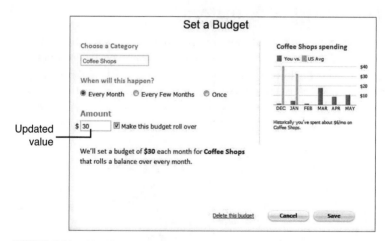

FIGURE 8.11   Modify an existing budget and click Save.

Figure 8.12 now shows that the updated budget item is no longer maxed out, giving me 20 more days to buy sweet tea and enjoy free Wi-Fi.

Auto & Transport: **Gas & Fuel**	**$135** *of* **$360**
Entertainment: **Movies & DVDs**	**$0** *of* **$20**
Food & Dining: **Alcohol & Bars**	**$0** *of* **$10**
Food & Dining: **Coffee Shops**	**$10** *of* **$30**
Food & Dining: **Fast Food**	**$68** *of* **$200**
Food & Dining: **Groceries**	**$336** *of* **$990**
Food & Dining: **Restaurants**	**$45** *of* **$250**
Shopping: **Books**	**$30** *of* **$100**
Shopping: **Clothing**	**$0** *of* **$270**

FIGURE 8.12   A modified budget with new value.

Deleting a Budget

In Figure 8.13 you see that Mint.com is monitoring my spending in the Alcohol & Bars category. My wife and I don't drink, so while this category is handy for verifying that my wife isn't hanging out at the local pub at happy hour, it's really not needed.

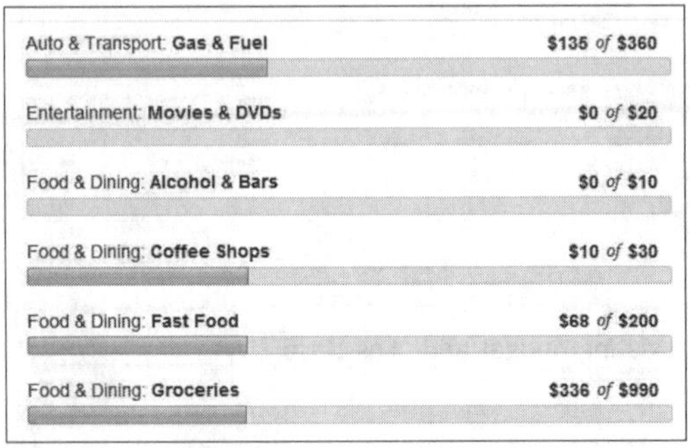

Auto & Transport: **Gas & Fuel**	**$135** *of* **$360**
Entertainment: **Movies & DVDs**	**$0** *of* **$20**
Food & Dining: **Alcohol & Bars**	**$0** *of* **$10**
Food & Dining: **Coffee Shops**	**$10** *of* **$30**
Food & Dining: **Fast Food**	**$68** *of* **$200**
Food & Dining: **Groceries**	**$336** *of* **$990**

FIGURE 8.13   Categories that are not relevant can be removed.

Removing a budget is even easier than editing one. Again, move your mouse pointer over the budget to be removed and click the Edit Details button. When the budget window opens, click the Delete This Budget link shown in Figure 8.14.

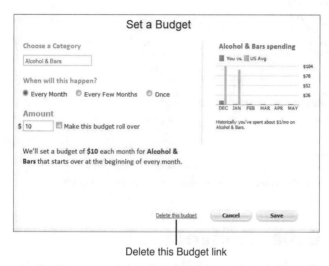

Delete this Budget link

FIGURE 8.14 Delete a budget to remove it from your monitored list.

TIP: **Deleted Budgets Still Available**

Choosing to delete a budget from your list of budget categories does not remove the budget forever. You can add it back anytime because it is still visible in the category list if you click the Add a Budget button. Mint.com is still able to calculate an average spending by scanning your account transactions.

Go back to your list of budget items, and you see that your deleted budget is removed from the list, as shown in Figure 8.15.

Auto & Transport: **Gas & Fuel**	**$135** *of* **$360**
Entertainment: **Movies & DVDs**	**$0** *of* **$20**
Food & Dining: **Coffee Shops**	**$10** *of* **$30**
Food & Dining: **Fast Food**	**$68** *of* **$200**
Food & Dining: **Groceries**	**$336** *of* **$990**
Food & Dining: **Restaurants**	**$45** *of* **$250**
Shopping: **Books**	**$30** *of* **$100**
Shopping: **Clothing**	**$0** *of* **$270**
▶ **Everything Else**	**$2,264** ○

FIGURE 8.15　Deleted budgets disappear from your monitored list.

View Other Budgets

Mint.com displays only the most active budgets and the budgets you have created in the monitored list. To view other budget items that Mint.com tracks, you need to scroll down and click the Everything Else link shown in Figure 8.16.

The list of budgets that become visible are typically budgets that don't see a lot of activity (meaning you might want to delete them or reduce the amount assigned). Figure 8.17 shows the list. You click the + sign to the right of each budget to access the screen to adjust its settings.

Using the Budgets Tool

After you've gone through your list of budget items and properly config-ured them with realistic values (you hope), how exactly do you use the Budgets tool?

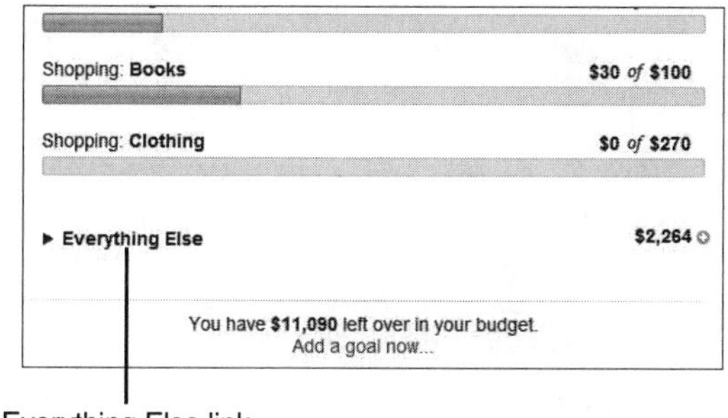

Everything Else link

FIGURE 8.16   Other budget categories are hidden from view.

Click + to edit

FIGURE 8.17   Other budget categories are hidden from view.

The first and most common usage is combining your budget settings with the Alerts feature (see Lesson 6, "Alerts") to receive emails (and SMS/text messages if you've configured it; again, see Lesson 6 for details) that alert you when you've gone over a specified budget. Figure 8.18 shows that I configured the Alerts feature to send me an email if I exceed any budget amounts. (So when I hit that $101 mark this month on book purchases, I can look forward to an email letting me know. If my wife is smart, she'll ask me to put her email address in the secondary email address field and get the same alert!)

Check boxes
to receive alerts

FIGURE 8.18   Use the Alerts feature to get emails and text messages when a budget amount is exceeded.

The next way I can use the budget feature is to see how much money I have left over after I assign values to all those items I want to track. To do this, I click the Budgets tab (on the Overview page) and look to the right side of the Budgets page at the running calculation shown in Figure 8.19.

Look closely at Figure 8.19 and understand exactly what these values mean. The first, Income, is easy—this is how much money Mint.com determines you are bringing in each month based on deposits. You can verify this by clicking the Edit Details button for the Paycheck category, also shown in Figure 8.19, and modify it if you know of other sources of income that aren't being properly flagged by Mint.com as income.

The next item, Spending, is a total of all the budget values you have set to this point. So if I have only three budget items of Gas, Food, and Rent and assign values of $200, $300, and $400, respectively, my Spending value will show $900.00.

Income versus Spending

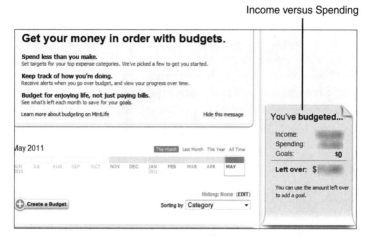

Get your money in order with budgets.

Spend less than you make.
Set targets for your top expense categories. We've picked a few to get you started.

Keep track of how you're doing.
Receive alerts when you go over budget, and view your progress over time.

Budget for enjoying life, not just paying bills.
See what's left each month to save for your goals.

Learn more about budgeting on MintLife   Hide this message

You've **budgeted...**

Income:
Spending:
Goals: $0

Left over: $

You can use the amount left over
to add a goal.

May 2011   This Month Last Month This Year All Time

JUN   JUL   AUG   SEP   OCT   NOV   DEC   JAN   FEB   MAR   APR   MAY
2010   2011

Hiding: None (EDIT)

Create a Budget   Sorting by Category   ▼

FIGURE 8.19   Get an estimate of how much money is left over.

The third item, Goals, likely shows a value of $0 unless you tinker with the Goals tab (or jump ahead to Lesson 9). Lesson 9 covers Goals, but think of them as similar to a private piggy bank that you set aside (or that spare mattress in the guest bedroom), and any money placed in it is off limits and will be deducted from the Income value.

The final item, Left Over, might make you leap for joy at first when you see how much free money you have in your accounts! Sorry to disappoint, but this value does not necessarily reflect how much money you actually have in your checking account; it means only that the value Mint.com has identified as your monthly income has not been completely divided up among various budget items. I might have a monthly expense of $500 that goes to Big John's Handyman Service for lawn and gutter cleaning services; however, if I haven't budgeted for that by increasing my Lawn & Garden budget category by $500, this Left Over value will fool me every time. If you make sure to set your budgets as accurately as possible, then and only then can you trust the Left Over value to properly reflect what's approximately left over in your cash accounts.

Another way to use the Budgets tool is to sort your budgets according to your spending. In Figure 8.20, you can see that if you select the Sorting By drop-down menu to Amount: High to Low, your budget list is reordered to show you where the largest spending occurs. This may pick up budgets that normally show up in the Everything Else list. You can likewise sort your budget list with Low to High spending.

Sort options for budgets

FIGURE 8.20   Sort your budget by spending level.

TIP: **Selecting Multiple Dates**

You can select individual months by clicking on the month you want to view or you can hold down the mouse button as you drag over multiple months to select a larger range of viewable data.

Finally, you can also view your budget list using data totaled for the current year. Figure 8.21 shows how clicking the This Year sorting option will add up budget categories for all the months of the current year and also show you total spending (versus total budgeting) for each category.

FIGURE 8.21   View an entire year's worth of budget data.

Summary

Budgeting is a useful feature that Mint.com offers to help you better understand random spending habits. It also allows users to predefine an amount of money to be set aside for known expenditures. Combining day-to-day spending habits with known expenditures provides users with a more accurate value for available cash, which is useful for recreational spending or for assigning to Goals, covered next in Lesson 9.

LESSON 9

Goals

In this lesson, you learn how to use Mint.com's Goals tool to create financial goals for big purchases (such as a home or car), trips, and funds (such as retirement or college). You learn how to create, edit, delete, and monitor goals, both custom and those already configured by Mint.com.

Setting Financial Goals

Mint.com is not only able to help you monitor your spending habits using the Budgets tool (see Lesson 8, "Budgets"), but it can also help you develop savings habits. You can open and link to a savings account, but any money found in a savings account is simply added to the Cash total on the Overview page.

Where Mint.com can help you increase your savings is by allowing you to create financial goals and keep them front and center, bringing them to your attention every time you log in (and even with email or text alerts).

Take a look at Figure 9.1. You see that I currently have no goals defined in the Goals section of the Overview page. That's about to change.

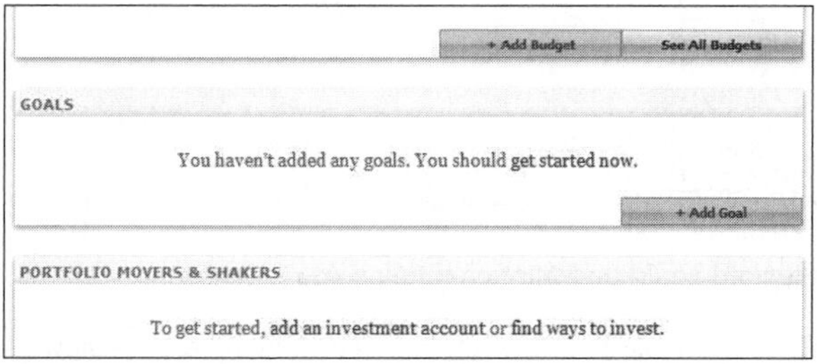

FIGURE 9.1 Mint.com users initially start with no financial goals.

Adding a Goal

There are two ways to create financial goals. The first is to click the Add Goal button indicated in Figure 9.1. The second method is to click the Goals tab on the Overview page toolbar, as indicated in Figure 9.2.

Goals tab

FIGURE 9.2   Select the Goals tab to create a new financial goal.

Either method takes you to the Goals page shown in Figure 9.3. Each of the boxes shown indicates a goal that Mint.com helps you set up and track.

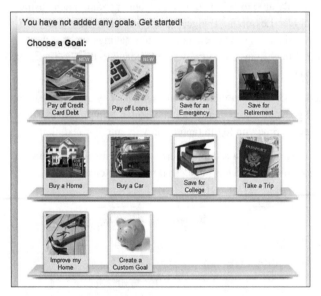

FIGURE 9.3   Predefined goals that Mint.com helps you reach.

Take a look at all the available goals; Mint.com occasionally creates new ones (the New tag identifies them) but you can create your own goal if you don't see it listed on the Goals page.

Let's first see how to use a predefined goal. After you understand how the Goals tool works, you can then create a custom goal.

Use a Mint.com Goal

Currently, Mint.com provides nine predefined goals: Pay Off Credit Card Debt, Pay Off Loans, Save for an Emergency, Save for Retirement, Buy a Home, Buy a Car, Save for College, Take a Trip, and Improve My Home. (We cover the Create a Custom Goal option in the next section.)

Clicking any of these nine goals will cause Mint.com to walk you through a unique process with questions and information requests that differ depending on which goal you select. We can't cover all of them here, and some of them may not even be relevant to you. (If you're a homeowner already or have just purchased a car, the Buy a Home and Buy a Car buttons will likely be of no interest to you—at least for a while.)

Even if a particular goal isn't relevant right now (such as Save for College for newlyweds with no children), you are still encouraged to click the goals and see what kinds of information you are asked to provide. You may find that some goals require a substantial amount of time to properly fund (such as college or retirement), so the sooner you create these goals the sooner you see results.

A few of the goals, however, can be used over and over and are not as "demanding" of your finances. For example, let's walk through setting a goal of taking a vacation next year (in 14 months to be exact) to Hawaii.

First, click the Take a Trip button. Figure 9.4 shows the window that appears to get us started on setting this particular financial goal.

What's great about the Mint.com Goals tool is that you likely encounter requests for information that you haven't really thought about yet. For example, in Figure 9.4 the Take a Trip screen is asking me for the number of days the trip will last. My wife and I haven't really given that much thought, but Mint.com is absolutely correct that to properly save, we really need to know exactly how many days (and nights) we plan to be gone.

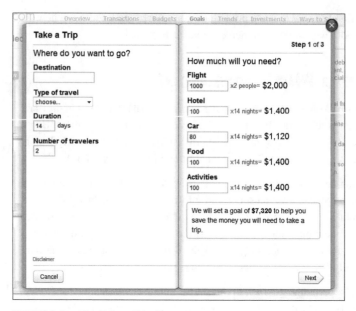

FIGURE 9.4   The Take a Trip financial goal starting screen.

Figure 9.5 shows that I provided some of the requested information but not everything yet.

The first thing to notice is that Mint.com provides some estimated travel costs on the right side that cover airfare, hotel, food, and other expenses. My wife has just informed me that 10 days may be longer than we can be away, so I change the duration to 7 days. Watch carefully—Figure 9.6 shows what happens so fast you might miss it.

Did you see it? Expenses that are likely to be affected by the change in duration are briefly highlighted and the total cost for the trip is adjusted.

Compare Figure 9.5 to Figure 9.6, and you see that Mint.com tells me that the total cost for a 10-day trip to Hawaii is around $5,800 for two people and $4,660 if I reduce the duration to 7 days.

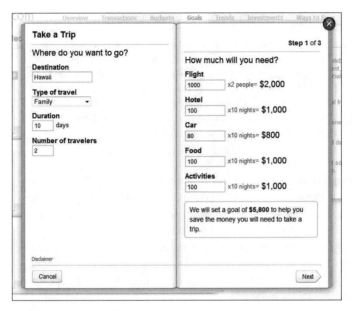

FIGURE 9.5   Just getting started in planning a vacation trip.

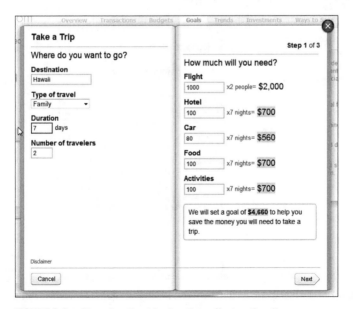

FIGURE 9.6   Changing the trip duration affects other items.

TIP: **Type of Trip**

You may think that the drop-down menu to select the Type of Trip (Spa, Romance, Golf, and so on) affects the overall cost, but Mint.com doesn't seem to think so. But you may agree that a 7-day trip to Hawaii to play golf every day is likely to be a bit more expensive than just spending 7 days lounging at the beach (all other things—hotel, airfare, food—being equal). Take the estimate that Mint.com gives you as a starting point only.

One thing you might notice is that Mint.com fills in many fields for you; the Flight, Hotel, Car, Food, and Activities boxes all contain pregenerated values. Luckily, these values are just suggestions. You can easily change these fields, and you should do so! For example, on our trip we plan to stay with some friends who have an extra car we can drive while we're there. So, Figure 9.7 shows that I change the Car amount to $10 (per day or night) to cover fuel. (I'm not going to leave my friends with an empty gas tank when we leave.)

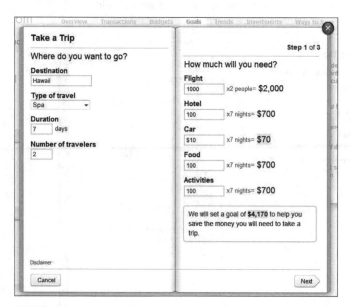

FIGURE 9.7   Changing one of the trip's expenses changes the overall cost.

> **CAUTION: Mint Is Not a Travel Service**
>
> Mint.com does not provide you with the ability to find good deals on things such as airfare and hotel. (And that's okay with me—plenty of Internet-based services such as kayak.com and priceline.com can find me the best prices on travel expenses.)

Next, I want to adjust the hotel expense. I found a nice hotel near our friends that costs $85.00 per night, and the airfare I found (assuming I travel in two months and the cost is equivalent 12 months from now) totals $743.00 round trip (per person). Figure 9.8 shows my updated goal details.

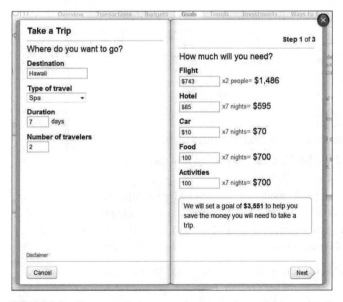

FIGURE 9.8   The overall trip costs change as I provide more details.

That's about all the information I can provide now. If I find that something changes, such as the cost of the hotel, I can go back at any time and modify a goal (more on how to do this shortly).

To continue with the Goals tool, you want to click the Next button, which takes you to Step 2 (of 3) and provides a screen like the one shown in Figure 9.9.

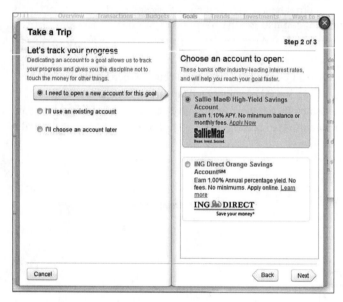

FIGURE 9.9   Step 2 of the Take a Trip goal creation.

The next step asks me how I plan to pay for the trip. I have three options: the first is to open an account (maybe a savings account) and the second is to use an existing account (that's linked to Mint.com). The third option is to skip this step and specify the method of payment later.

I choose an existing account, so I select the second option, as shown in Figure 9.10.

One thing you need to understand right away is that specifying an existing account is not going to deduct that money from your account; remember that Mint.com can only view your financial data. You cannot transfer money or make payments, so setting a goal and telling Mint.com how you plan to pay for it is done only so that Mint.com can monitor your accounts to see when you move (transfer) funds or write a check to yourself for a specific goal.

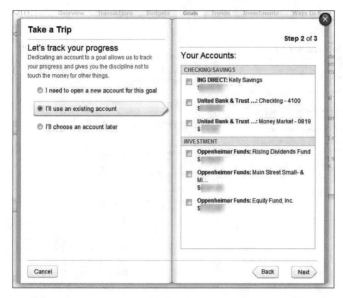

FIGURE 9.10   You can select an existing account to help pay for a goal.

Figure 9.11 shows that I select my savings (money market) account as the place where I put the funds needed for the vacation. I could just as easily select my checking accounts or even my investment accounts (although that wouldn't be a good idea, because those funds are tied to my retirement).

Now I click the Next button; Figure 9.12 shows Step 3 (of 3) that opens.

I'm asked to provide this goal with a unique title (name). Because I might plan another trip, a title will help me distinguish between the two. Figure 9.13 shows that I call this one "Big Kahuna."

You see in Figure 9.13 that I can revisit my estimates for the costs of the trip when I click the Re-estimate This Goal link. Likewise, I can click the account link specified in Figure 9.13 to change, for example, from my money market account to my checking account.

The other half of Step 3 allows me to specify the trip's date. This trip is set for July of 2012, so after I enter that information, Mint.com calculates how much money I should transfer into my money market account each month, as shown in Figure 9.14.

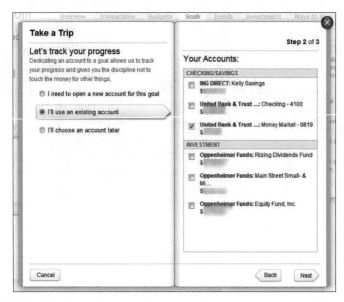

FIGURE 9.11   Select an account to use for a goal.

FIGURE 9.12   The Goal summary page.

Click to modify goal settings

FIGURE 9.13 Give your goal a name to make it easier to track.

FIGURE 9.14 Mint.com calculates monthly savings needed to fulfill a goal.

When you're done, click the Save Goal button. You are taken to a screen like the one in Figure 9.15 that lists all your goals and shows your progress when it comes to meeting a goal's financial requirements.

FIGURE 9.15   A progress bar shows you the status of a goal.

After you add a single goal, visiting the Goals tab always shows you the screen in Figure 9.15. If you want to add a new goal, click the Add a Goal button and select from the list of predefined goals or choose to create a custom goal.

One final item that might interest you is the Next Steps box shown at the right of your goals in Figure 9.15. The Next Steps box often provides you with links to services (either Mint.com services, such as the Budgets tool, or third-party services, such as member rewards cards) that might help with fulfilling a goal or at least saving some cash while enjoying a goal. Click a link in the Next Steps box to see where it takes you. You're under no obligation to sign up or use a service, so take a look. You never know what Mint.com might offer its users that could save you money or bring a goal closer to fulfillment.

Editing a Goal

After you create a goal (or even a dozen), it's a simple matter to update a goal's data (in the case of a trip, for example, the travel date may change or the airfare costs might go up). From the Goal's tab, move your mouse pointer over a goal and click the View Details button that appears, as shown in Figure 9.16.

Click to View Details

FIGURE 9.16 Edit a goal by first viewing its details.

The screen expands and provides you with summary information related to a goal. See Figure 9.17.

Click to edit the goal

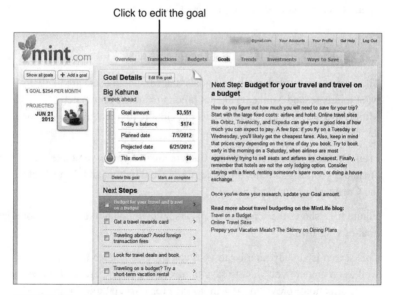

FIGURE 9.17 A goal's summary data appears along with other options.

Looking at Figure 9.17, you notice that along the bottom of the screen is the familiar Next Steps box with suggestions. Each item has a check box assigned to it that allows you to check off items as you complete them (or at least investigate certain options). To the right side of the screen you also find links to online articles from Mint.com's archives that often contain useful information related to a certain type of goal.

You click the Edit This Goal button to reopen the earlier windows (Steps 1, 2, and 3) and make changes. You can also click the Add a Goal button to create a new goal, or click the Delete This Goal button to permanently remove it from the Goals tab. One additional option is to tap the Mark as Complete button to indicate a goal has been reached (a trip taken, a house purchased, and so on).

If you don't want to edit the goal, delete the goal, or mark it as complete, click the Show All Goals button to return to the previous screen. Any changes you make to a goal (or recalculated totals) appear along with updates to the overall status of your goal's fulfillment.

Creating a Custom Goal

There are an unlimited number of goals that Mint.com users are likely to want to create, and Mint.com cannot predict them all. Fortunately, Mint.com gives you the Create a Custom Goal button that allows you to define your own special goal.

From the Goals tab, click Create a Custom Goal if you haven't already created a goal; if you have, click the Add a Goal button, and then select the Create a Custom Goal button.

Figure 9.18 shows the screen that appears, allowing you to create a unique goal of your own.

This screen is already familiar to you; you provide a name for the goal, as well as an amount you want to save to meet the goal. Figure 9.19 shows the information I provided—I want to save for a special tool for my workshop and have entered the price of the item. I even uploaded an image of the item for motivation to save.

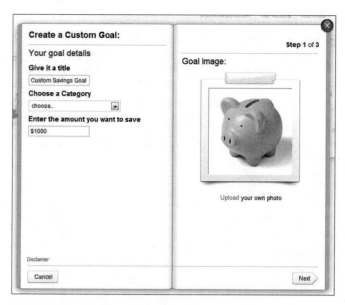

FIGURE 9.18   Creating a unique goal starts out like any other goal.

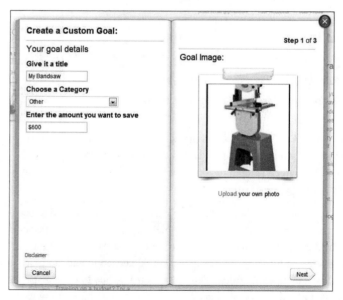

FIGURE 9.19   Give your custom goal a name and a financial goal to reach.

Click the Next button. Figure 9.20 shows Step 2 to create a custom goal. It's a familiar screen where you need to specify an account to hold the funds. Notice in the figure that my money market account is grayed out; there aren't enough funds in it to meet both my original Take a Trip goal and now my custom goal. I can open a new account with a suggested third-party service, as shown on the right, or I can choose another account.

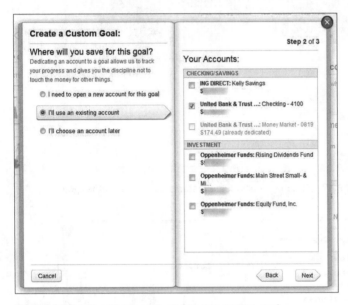

FIGURE 9.20   Specify an account for your custom goal.

For now, I decide to leave my checking account as the account that supplies the funds for my custom goal and click the Next button. Figure 9.21 shows the final screen (Step 3 of 3) where I specify the date I plan to purchase the item.

I want to buy it in December of 2011, so Mint.com tells me I need to set aside approximately $86.00 per month to meet my goal. However, because I use a checking account that has a balance of at least the cost of the item, Mint.com tells me that I've met the goal with $0 needed to add, and the progress bar is completely filled. This changes if I decide to open a special account just to hold the money I need to save for the purchase of my tool.

FIGURE 9.21 View the summary screen for your custom goal.

I click the Save Goal button and the custom goal is now listed on the Goals tab along with my Take a Trip goal, as shown in Figure 9.22.

Goals are also listed on the Overview page, so when you log in to Mint.com, you get a quick list of the goals you want to reach.

Finally, if you want to receive text messages or email alerts when you meet a goal, click the Your Accounts link (in the upper-right corner of the screen) and then select the Email & Alerts tab, as shown in Figure 9.23.

Place a check mark in the box for either email or SMS (or both) to receive one very welcome message that you met a special goal, and then give yourself a big pat on the back.

FIGURE 9.22   The new custom goal is added to the list of goals.

Check boxes to receive alerts related to goals

FIGURE 9.23   Get an alert email or text message when you fulfill a goal.

Summary

Having Mint.com track your goals is a great motivator to save money (or to use the Budgets tool) for special purchases, trips, or funds (such as college or retirement). Mint.com makes it easy to create as many goals as you need to keep you motivated and help you find ways to increase your savings and decrease spending.

LESSON 10

Trends & Ways to Save

In this lesson, you learn how to use two Mint.com features, Trends and Ways to Save, to identify your spending and saving habits, investment returns, and areas where you can save more money.

At its most basic level, Mint.com allows you to link to your various accounts—checking, savings, investment, mortgage, and so on—and view a simplified summary on the Overview page, keeping all the details of the numerous transactions hidden away until you want to examine them. That level of service is probably all that a large portion of Mint.com users require.

But Mint.com offers some additional features to those users who have completed their profiles and linked Mint.com to all their various account types.

The first feature introduced in this lesson is Mint.com's Trends feature. This feature enables you to select various aspects of your financial life and generate easy-to-understand charts and lists that can help you get an even better understanding of your spending, saving, and investing.

The second feature you learn about is the Ways to Save tool. You can use this to compare new services, such as credit cards, loans, and more (as well as their interest rates and fees), against the services you already use.

These two features are found on the Overview page's toolbar, as shown in Figure 10.1.

FIGURE 10.1   Trends and Ways to Save are part of the Mint.com toolbar.

Let's take a look at the Trends tool and then look at how the Ways to Save tool can possibly help you find some better deals than the ones you may be currently using.

Trends

From the Overview page, click the Trends tab. You see a screen open similar to the one in Figure 10.2.

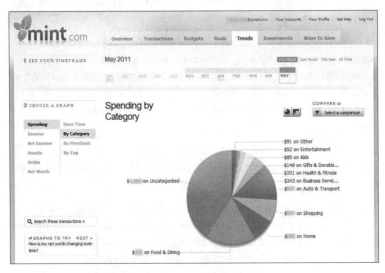

FIGURE 10.2 The Trends page has multiple steps.

Scroll down the page and then back up—you may notice that the page is broken into three sections: Set Your Timeframe, Choose a Graph, and Get the Report.

Let's start with the Set the Timeframe section shown in Figure 10.3.

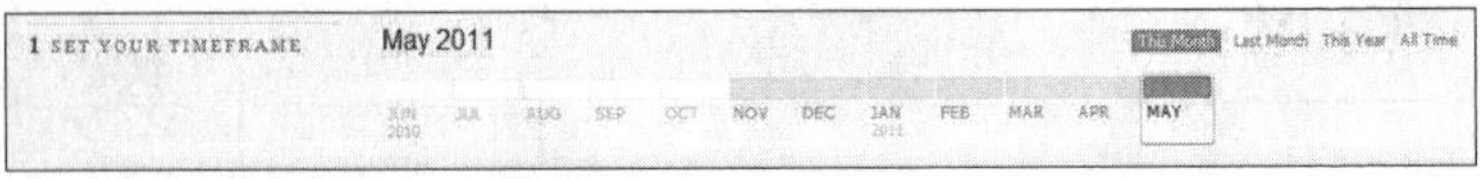

FIGURE 10.3 Start with the Set Your Timeframe section.

Trends provides you with custom reports on various aspects of your financial life. You can get reports on where your money is spent, how your income level changes, and even learn how you compare in certain areas to the rest of the country (such as spending on fuel costs).

You first must select a time period. You can click a specific month, or click and hold your mouse button and drag over a series of months, as shown in Figure 10.4. You can also click selections such as Last Month, This Month, This Year, and All Time.

FIGURE 10.4   Select the time period you want to examine.

After selecting a month or series of months, you next move to the Choose a Graph section. You have six Trend options here: Spending, Income, Net Income, Assets, Debts, and Net Worth. Selecting one of the six Trend options makes available a short list of suboptions. Figure 10.5, for example, shows that I selected Spending as my main Trend option and then I selected the By Category suboption.

FIGURE 10.5   Choose a Graph option to create custom charts.

Figure 10.6 shows the custom graph that my data creates; notice that I selected the pie chart option, but I can easily switch over to a bar graph by toggling between the chart type buttons.

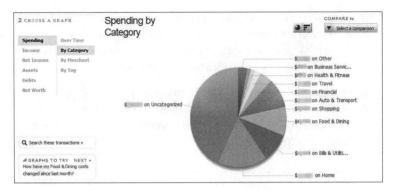

FIGURE 10.6   View your custom chart and toggle between pie and bar graph.

In the Choose a Graph section, you also see a set of hard-to-find graphs that you can access only when you click the Next link for the Graphs to Try section, shown in Figure 10.7.

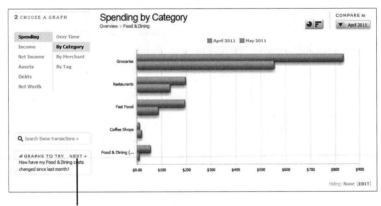

Click Next to cycle to next graph

FIGURE 10.7   View even more graphs with the Graphs to Try option.

Every time you click the Next link, the title of a graph changes. Figure 10.7 shows a link that, when clicked, opens a graph for "How have my food and dining costs changed since last month?" along with the matching chart.

After you select the time period you want to view and the type of graph you want to examine, you then move on to Step 3, the Get the Report section shown in Figure 10.8.

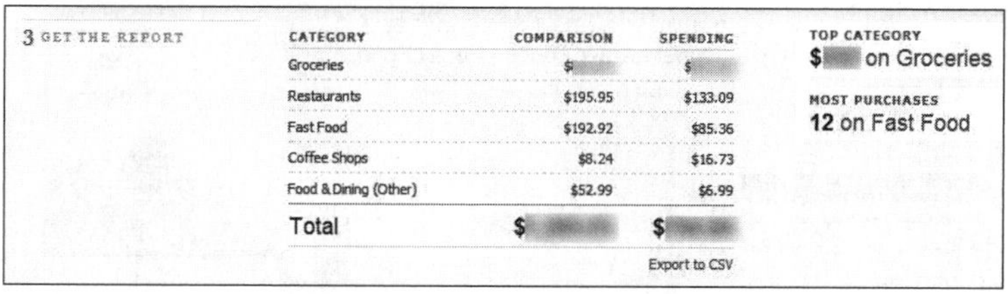

3 GET THE REPORT	CATEGORY	COMPARISON	SPENDING	TOP CATEGORY
	Groceries	$	$	$ ▮ on Groceries
	Restaurants	$195.95	$133.09	MOST PURCHASES
	Fast Food	$192.92	$85.36	12 on Fast Food
	Coffee Shops	$8.24	$16.73	
	Food & Dining (Other)	$52.99	$6.99	
	Total	$ ▮	$ ▮	
			Export to CSV	

FIGURE 10.8   Get the Report provides a summary of the visual data.

The Get the Report section changes as you select different time periods and different types of graphs. This section provides a summary of the pie or bar chart's data as well as a link to download the data to a CSV file.

Whether you choose to download a CSV file to use with a spreadsheet for performing more specific calculations (well, more specific than Mint.com can provide) or just use the Get the Report section to read over the results, you see that having both the visual chart (pie or bar graph) and the matching list of financial data makes it easier for you to track your accounts, your spending, and your saving. But what about investments, you ask? Mint.com has you covered.

Take a look at Figure 10.9. It shows the Investments page, reached when you click the Investments tab nestled between the Trends and the Ways to Save buttons.

FIGURE 10.9   The Investments tab provides visual feedback for just your investments.

The Investments tab works just like the Trends tab, but instead of various categories, you select the different investment accounts you linked to Mint.com. After you select an account (or click the All Investments link), you can select a time frame (1 day, 5 days, 1 month, 3 months, 6 months, and 1 year) as well as whether to view graphs based on performance over time, value, allocation, and performance against indicators, such as NAS-DAQ, Dow Jones, or S&P 500.

As with the Trends tab, the Investments tab requires you to invest time (not money) to properly understand all the features it offers. But after you discover how it works, you may find yourself checking it frequently as you watch your investments' performances over time.

Returning to the Trends tool, you'll find that it is most useful when you properly categorize all of your transactions (see Lesson 7, "Categories," for instructions on categorizing transactions). If you did this, you see that the Trends tool can help you discover how much money you spend on groceries versus fast food each month, for example. You can configure the graphs to show you how you divide your assets between cash and investments, what your credit card debt looks like compared to overall debt (that includes mortgages and car loans), and even view your Net Worth over time as your investments grow and your loan values decrease. You want to do all this so you can get a better grasp on your overall financial health, and that means you know where your money is spent, where it earns interest, and where it is saved.

Speaking of saving money, that's the next feature you learn about.

Ways to Save

Click the Ways to Save tab and you see the screen shown in Figure 10.10.

FIGURE 10.10 The Ways to Save tab offers 10 money-saving possibilities.

The first thing to do is determine which of the 10 money-saving categories apply to you. For example, if you don't have any credit cards (and don't want to have one), the Credit Cards tab shown in Figure 10.11 won't be of interest to you. Likewise, if you do not own a home or are not in the market for a home, the Home Loans tab won't be of any help to you, either.

FIGURE 10.11   Find the ways to save that are relevant to you.

Select the Checking tab to see how the Ways to Save feature works, but keep in mind that the process is almost identical for the remaining nine tabs. After selecting a tab, you get either an exact or estimated summary of your current situation at the top of the screen, as shown in Figure 10.12.

FIGURE 10.12   Select a tab to display your current financial data for that category.

For the checking category, for example, Mint.com tells me how much money, on average, I maintain as my balance for my current checking account. It also tells me that I earn 0% interest on that account.

Mint.com provides a set of filters that allow you to find similar services that might provide them at either a lower price or with a higher percentage rate. These filters are adjusted using the drag bars shown in Figure 10.13.

FIGURE 10.13   Use filters to find better service features.

Using the drag bars in Figure 10.13, I decide to look for a checking account that has no Minimum to Open fee (dragged to $0), no fees on balances less than $1,500, a monthly fee no greater than $15, and an annual percentage yield (APY) greater than 0.40%.

Figure 10.14 shows these filters set and the single bank that offers a checking account that meets my requirements.

FIGURE 10.14   Set your filters and see what offers are available.

If you find one or more services that meet your filter requirements, click the Apply button for the bank or financial institution you want to use and follow the onscreen instructions.

You may specify a set of service requirements that are impossible to meet; if you don't find any services that meet your filter requirements, you need to "lighten" your filters a bit until you find an institution that can offer what you want.

For example, by changing the APY to 0% in my filters, I increased my results from one to four as shown in Figure 10.15.

Adjust to 0%

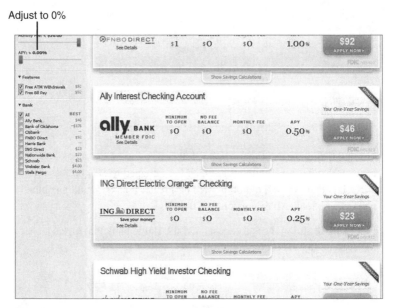

FIGURE 10.15   Changing just one filter item can increase your options.

You now see how you can use the Ways to Save tool to find a better checking account, but you have nine other categories to check out. Use the Auto Insurance, for example, to compare what you pay now to what rates you can obtain with a variety of other insurance companies.

You find that each of the 10 Ways to Save categories requests different types of information from you. Keep in mind that you're not obligated in any way to use any of the services that meet your filter requirements. Mint.com provides these only as stepping stones to "introduce" you to companies and financial institutions that try to save you money. Be smart, check out your options, do some research, ask questions if necessary, and make the right decisions for you, not for the organization that wants you to sign on the line.

Summary

It takes a lot of time to set up your Mint.com account so you can better understand your financial situation. Tools such as Trends and Ways to Save are additional features that Mint.com provides to give you even more information so you can make better decisions.

LESSON 11
Mobile Mint

In this lesson, you learn how to access and use Mint.com on mobile devices such as phones and tablets.

Take Mint.com with You

Mint.com is a browser-based service, so it's no surprise that you find the most up-to-date features and tools it has to offer when you power up your computer or laptop's web browser and point it to www.mint.com.

But we live in a mobile world. It's not always convenient to sit in front of a computer screen when you want to access your Mint.com account. Fortunately, Mint.com makes its services available to those users who have a smart phone (with the capability to download and use apps or open an app browser) or tablet with Wi-Fi connectivity or a data plan (3G/4G).

To start, we introduce you to a couple of the Mint.com apps available for both Android and iOS, the two most popular operating systems for mobile phones. (Other versions likely exist or will be released for Windows, Palm, Blackberry, and other brands of phones, so check with either the app market/store for your phone or Mint.com for details.)

Mint.com and Android

You can get the Mint.com app for Android when you visit the Android Market and search for Mint.com. Figure 11.1 shows the Mint.com app in the Android Market—just click the Free button to install the app.

FIGURE 11.1   Mint.com is found in the Android Market.

TIP: **Enable Security**

I require a code to be entered before turning on my phone, but if you don't do this (or lack the ability), you'll be happy to know that the Mint.com app will allow you to configure a four-digit passcode before opening the app. After installing and opening the app, tap the Menu button on your phone and choose Settings. Choose the first option, Use Passcode, and enter your four-digit number that must be entered every time the Mint.com app is opened.

After you install the app, it appears in the Application folder, as shown in Figure 11.2.

Tap the Mint.com Android app and log in with your Mint.com email address and password, as shown in Figure 11.3.

Mint.com app

FIGURE 11.2 The Mint.com app is installed and stored in the Application folder.

Keep in mind that the Mint.com apps are designed to run on the smaller screens of a mobile device, so the information it provides is limited compared to what you see on a larger computer or laptop.

Figure 11.4 shows the app's Overview screen, where you find the current cash balance, credit card debt amount, alerts, and a few other features.

Tap the small arrow to the right of any item to see more details related to that section of the screen. Figure 11.5 shows that after I tap the small arrow for the Cash and Credit Card debt balances, I get a more detailed breakdown of my checking, savings, credit card, and investment accounts. (You have to scroll up and down to view everything—Mint.com tries to fit as much as possible on the small screen, but there are limits.)

Use your Android phone's Back or Return button to return to a previous screen.

FIGURE 11.3 Log in to Mint.com with your email and password.

FIGURE 11.4 The Mint.com app's Overview screen.

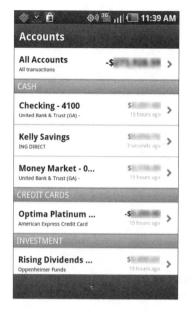

FIGURE 11.5 Get more details on various Mint.com app items.

On the Overview screen, you may see a small number to the right of the Alerts item. This lets you know how many alerts Mint.com has flagged for your attention. You can see in Figure 11.4 that I have three alerts that I can view when I tap the small arrow to the right of the Alerts item.

The Budget item allows you to view how much you spent on various categories (to set up the Budgets feature, see Lesson 8, "Budgets"). Figure 11.6 shows that I spent $17 of my $30 monthly budget and have $13 remaining.

Remember that anytime you see an arrow to the right of an item or category, that means Mint.com can provide more details. For example, refer to Figure 11.5 to see an arrow to the right of my Checking account. By tapping that arrow, I can view individual charges (from my debit card) and checks that have cleared in a scrollable list, as shown in Figure 11.7.

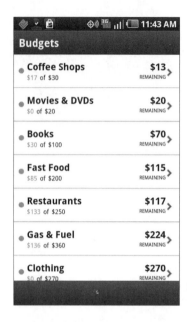

FIGURE 11.6   Check the Budgets feature to see your expenditures.

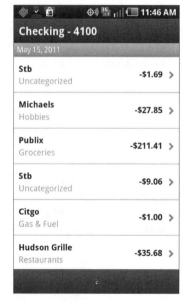

FIGURE 11.7   View checking account transactions.

If I tap a transaction's arrow (such as the Stb expense of $1.69 shown in Figure 11.7), I go to a screen like the one shown in Figure 11.8. Notice that every detail here has its own arrow. I can tap the Description field's arrow, for example, and edit the name—changing Stb to Coffee Shop. I can also tap the arrow next to the Category field and assign this to a category for budgeting and tracking purposes. Finally, I can tap the arrow to the right of the Notes field and add my own text if I want.

FIGURE 11.8   Edit transaction details such as name and category.

As you can see, the Mint.com for the Android operating system has many of the same features available from a web browser. You just have to know where to look and tap a few extra places to find them.

Not all features are available, but keep on the lookout for updates. Mint.com is likely to continue to improve the app as more and more users move to mobile phones for their computing needs.

Mint.com and iOS

Mint.com is also available as an app for those mobile devices running Apple's iOS—this means the iPhone and the iTouch.

After you install the app to your device, tap the app to open it and log in on a screen like the one shown in Figure 11.9.

FIGURE 11.9   Log in to the iOS app version of Mint.com

After you log in, you'll find that the app works just like the Android version. Figure 11.10 shows the Overview screen with identical sections showing Cash and Credit Card balances, Alerts, Budget data, and more.

As with the Android app, the small arrows to the right of different sections of the screen, when tapped, open up more details. Figure 11.11, for example, shows one Mint.com user's Budget information.

FIGURE 11.10 The iOS Mint.com version's Overview screen.

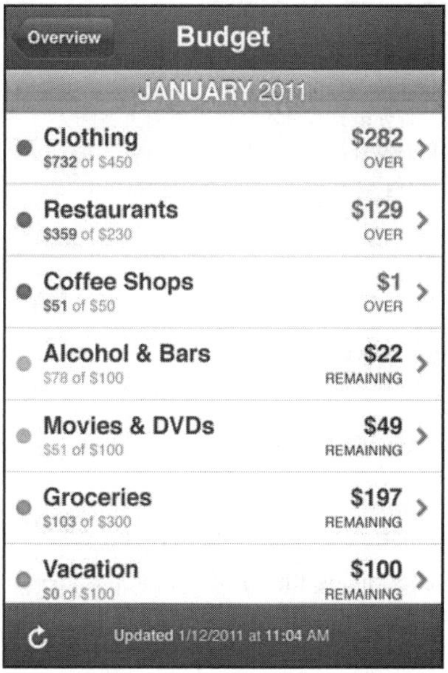

FIGURE 11.11 Budget information on the iOS Mint.com app.

Whether you choose to install either the iOS or Android version of the
Mint.com app, you'll likely find that it's a helpful tool for keeping up-to-
date with your financial information. For me, it's so much easier to open
the Mint.com app, log in, and check to see whether a check has cleared or
a deposit went through than it is to log in to my bank's online banking
tool. While I'm in the Mint.com app, I can also check on things such as
how my investments are doing, whether there has been any unusual activity (via the Alerts option), and how my spending habits are stacking up
this month.

Mint.com and Tablets

A number of tablets are available today, including the iPad, the Motorola
Xoom, and many more. Currently, no Mint.com apps exist specifically for
a tablet, and the reason for this is simple—tablets typically come with a
web browser that is fully capable of accessing the full version of
Mint.com.

TIP: **Mint.com Apps for Smaller Screen Tablets**

Android tablets with smaller screens, such as the Samsung Galaxy
Tab (with its 7-inch screen), do better running the same app that is
available for Android mobile phones. You can download the free
app from the Android Market and install it on the Galaxy Tab. The
screens are identical to those covered earlier in this lesson, but
larger.

Figure 11.12, for example, shows the Mint.com website as viewed on an
iPad.

Figure 11.13 shows Mint.com running on the Motorola Xoom's Browser
app.

Mint.com works great on tablets, especially those with the larger screen,
such as the iPad and the Xoom. However, using the Mint.com app on a
tablet does require either a Wi-Fi or data connection.

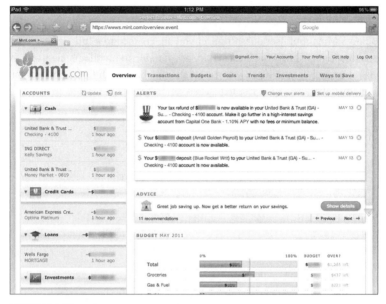

FIGURE 11.12 Mint.com on the Apple iPad.

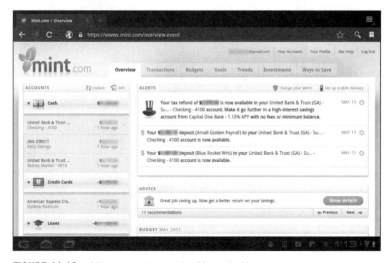

FIGURE 11.13 Mint.com runs on the Motorola Xoom.

Summary

Being a Mint.com user doesn't mean you are chained to a full-size computer or laptop. The Mint.com service is available to mobile phone users via a free app as well as on various tablets that have an Internet connection and a web browser app installed.

LESSON 12

Educate Yourself (Blog/Forum Usage)

In this lesson, you learn about additional resources available to you as a Mint.com user. You learn about Mint.com's forums as well as its blog, and resources available to users who have questions or just want to learn more about various financial topics.

The Mint.com Community

Although this book attempts to provide the best overview of the basic Mint.com services, you may still have questions about more advanced topics, or you may be looking for more assistance with the basic services or details on how to make Mint.com work harder for you.

Mint.com doesn't just provide the financial services covered in previous lessons and leave its users with a technical support phone number or email address. Rather, Mint.com provides a handful of other features that are accessible from the www.mint.com site, including the Frequently Asked Questions screen (called the Help page) where you can ask questions and find immediate answers. You also find a great discussion forum area to post questions (the ones not answered by the Help page), get responses from Mint.com employees and other Mint.com users, and share your own experiences with other users who may have questions to which you may know the answer.

In addition to the discussion forums, there are a large collection of articles related to various financial subjects (insurance, mortgage, retirement, college planning, and more) and a blog that is frequently updated with the latest financial news that is helpful to Mint.com users.

Frequently Asked Questions

One of the first places you should start when you have a question about Mint.com is the Help page's FAQ, or Frequently Asked Questions. You access it from the Overview page when you click the Get Help link indicated at the top of the screen in Figure 12.1.

Get Help link

FIGURE 12.1   Get Help on the Overview page.

The Help page has different sections for you to examine (I cover them all shortly), but I want you to scroll down the page a little bit and focus on the list of Frequently Asked Questions, shown in Figure 12.2.

Frequently Asked Questions

My financial institution is supported by Mint but I can't add it. What should I do?

I'm having problems with the security challenge when adding my account.

I can't find my bank, credit card or financial institution.

What should I do if my bank is not supported?

Does Mint.com support international banks?

Can I input my cash transactions?

How do I manually add cash transactions and pending checks?

How can I make a product suggestion?

I am experiencing a problem. How should I submit a bug?

How is Mint.com free?

If I submit a request via the contact form, how long will it take to get a response?

FIGURE 12.2   Scan the FAQ list to see if your question is there.

The list of questions shown in Figure 12.2 is selected by Mint.com as representative of the most common questions from users. If your question is on the list, great! Click the question and a drop-down box appears with a solution to your problem or an answer to your question.

Figure 12.3 shows a couple of responses to two of the common questions.

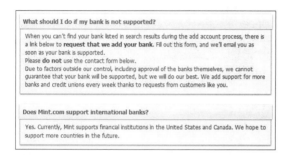

What should I do if my bank is not supported?

When you can't find your bank listed in search results during the add account process, there is a link below to **request that we add your bank**. Fill out this form, and we'll email you as soon as your bank is supported.
Please **do not** use the contact form below.
Due to factors outside our control, including approval of the banks themselves, we cannot guarantee that your bank will be supported, but we will do our best. We add support for more banks and credit unions every week thanks to requests from customers like you.

Does Mint.com support international banks?

Yes. Currently, Mint supports financial institutions in the United States and Canada. We hope to support more countries in the future.

FIGURE 12.3   Quick responses are provided for the most frequently asked questions.

But what should you do if your question isn't on the list? Easy—scroll back to the top of the screen and type your question into the text box, as shown in Figure 12.4. Be sure to also provide a shorter title for the question before clicking the Continue button.

Ask a question

    Idea   **Question**   **Problem**   Praise

How do I export my financial data to a spreadsheet?

Export to Spreadsheet

Continue   POWERED BY **satisfaction**

Include a question title

FIGURE 12.4   Enter your own question if it's not found on the FAQ list.

A short list of possible answers is provided, as shown in Figure 12.5. As you can see, the handful of questions there don't answer my question.

Before you post, see if people are already talking about something similar.

Your question:
Export to Spreadsheet

Questions already posted in the community:

🔎 **export mint transaction data to MS Money**
I would like to export info from my various brokerage accounts to Microsoft Money .ofx format. Th...

💬 **When will we be able to import data exported from financial institutions that don'...**
I love Mint but unfortunately I can't import some of my financial data. I assume this has someth...

💬 **Shared Bank Accounts Showing Twice in Mint**
We've seen a great deal of reports of duplicate accounts from users who share bank accounts with ...

💬 **Why do I have an inactive account?**
We are transitioning off our old data provider to our internal data provider, and have been in pr...

See all 1000 search results

None of t ese fit, post my question   Or Go back

Click for more results

FIGURE 12.5   Your question may or may not be answered.

My question wasn't answered, so I click the See All 1000 Results link (indicated in Figure 12.5). Figure 12.6 shows the page that opens to display more possible answers.

A good match

Community | ▸   Search / Topics

408 topics found for "Export to Spreadsheet"

💬 Everything   💡 Questions   💡 Ideas   ⚠ Problems   💬 Praise   🔄 Updates

Is there a way to export my transactions to Excel?
I just want to be able to have a **spreadsheet** on my laptop for the times I don't have internet access. Is there any way to download or **export** data from Mint to my laptop? (2011-02-11)
TAGS: **export** download excel csv
💬 · Answered · 10 replies · ☆ 4

💬 You can download them all to microsoft works **spreadsheet** and then open in excel. Go to transactions and at the bottom of the page in fine print it says **export** all xxxx transactions. (2011-02-11)

Exported Transactions Should Have Unique ID
EXPORTED TRANSACTIONS SHOULD HAVE UNIQUE ID I regularly **export** my transactions from the transactions page so I can import them into a **spreadsheet** and run different reports on them. However, when mint updates the description or category of a transaction, ... (2011-04-12)
TAGS: **export**, transaction, csv, duplicate, **spreadsheet**
💬

FIGURE 12.6   Examine additional possible answers to your question.

I got lucky and found that the very first response in the list in Figure 12.6 is exactly what I'm looking for—exporting my data to an Excel spreadsheet. Figure 12.7 shows a couple responses to an identical question.

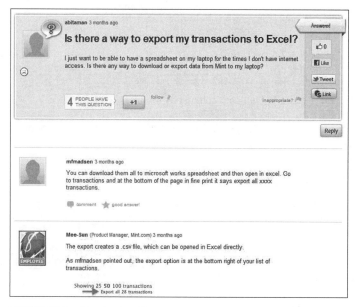

FIGURE 12.7   Read other Mint.com user responses to a question.

The page shown in Figure 12.7 has a lot of features. You can read all the responses to a question, see whether the responses were accepted (by the original Mint.com user who posted the question), and even add your own comments to the page.

But what do you do if you still cannot find the answer you need? It's time to take your question to the Mint.com forums.

The Mint.com Community Forums

To visit the forums, you can either click the Community link indicated in Figure 12.8 or point your web browser to http://satisfaction.mint.com.

Click to go to forums

FIGURE 12.8   Visit the Mint.com community forums.

Whichever method you choose, you arrive at the Mint.com forums' home page shown in Figure 12.9.

FIGURE 12.9   The Mint.com Community Forum home page.

You're already logged in to Mint.com, so you can post your question using the Ask a Question text box, as shown in Figure 12.10, and then click the Continue button to submit it.

You receive a short list of questions that Mint.com believes may be similar to the one you submitted. If you see one, click it—otherwise, click the Nope, Finish Posting My Question button, as shown in Figure 12.11.

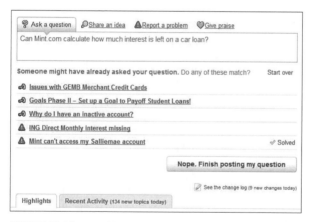

Community-powered support for Mint.com
Supported by 180,923 customers like you, as well as the Mint.com team.

Community | ▸ / Overview

❓ Ask a question   🖉 Share an idea   ⚠ Report a problem   ♡ Give praise

Can Mint.com calculate how much interest is left on a car loan?

Ask a question. We'll see if other people have this idea, too.   **Continue**   Start over

See the change log (9 new changes today)

Highlights   Recent Activity (134 new topics today)

❓ FREQUENTLY ASKED QUESTIONS

Why is my bank account in an error state?
Traycee asked · 524 replies · Last reply 6 hours ago by abarnetson   ☆ **452**

FIGURE 12.10   Ask your question and then submit it.

❓ Ask a question   🖉 Share an idea   ⚠ Report a problem   ♡ Give praise

Can Mint.com calculate how much interest is left on a car loan?

Someone might have already asked your question. Do any of these match?   Start over

💬 **Issues with GEMB Merchant Credit Cards**

💬 **Goals Phase II – Set up a Goal to Payoff Student Loans!**

💬 **Why do I have an inactive account?**

⚠ **ING Direct Monthly interest missing**

⚠ **Mint can't access my Salliemae account**   ✔ Solved

Nope. Finish posting my question

See the change log (9 new changes today)

Highlights   Recent Activity (134 new topics today)

FIGURE 12.11   Look for matches or choose to submit your question.

The Start a New Topic page opens. Provide more details in the Add Some Details text box, as shown in Figure 12.12, and then click the Post button.

TIP: Don't Share Your Email Address

Be sure to uncheck the check box shown in Figure 12.12 that asks whether you'd like to share your email address with other Mint.com users. Use the forum for your questions and don't share your email address; I can think of no reason to provide your email address to strangers when you simply need an answer to a Mint.com question.

Add more details

Click to Post

FIGURE 12.12   Provide more details and post your question.

If this is your first time to post a question to the Mint.com forum, you receive an email with a verification code and you must provide it (plus create a new password for the forum) before posting your question, as shown in Figure 12.13.

Log into the Mint.com forum to find your question posted and ready for others to provide assistance. Figure 12.14 shows my question posted on the forum.

After you post your question, the waiting game begins. Sometimes you receive a response within minutes of posting, and other times you may have to wait hours or even days for a response.

FIGURE 12.13   Enter a verification code and password to use the forum.

FIGURE 12.14   Your question is posted and waiting for responses.

The forum has many more features available: search tools, access to Mint.com employees, the capability to flag questions for later reading, and the option to tag questions with keywords that make topics easier to find during a search at a later time. I highly encourage you to spend some time investigating all the forum tools and options.

The forum is definitely a great place to post unique questions that you may have about the Mint.com services, but there's another place you can go when you want to learn more about how Mint.com can help you—a blog that is updated regularly with articles of interest to users.

Mint.com Blog

The folks at Mint.com want to attract more users to the service, and one way they do this (in addition to providing a great set of free financial services) is to provide users with useful information that can help make more money, save more money, and just make better financial decisions.

They provide this information for free on the Mint.com blog that you can access by pointing your browser to www.mint.com/blog. You can also log out of your Mint.com account, scroll to the bottom of the screen to the list of other Mint.com services, and click the Personal Finance Blog link indicated in Figure 12.15.

Personal Finance Blog

FIGURE 12.15   Visit the Personal Finance Blog for useful articles.

> TIP: **Spend Some Time on the Mint.com Home Page**
>
> When you're not logged into Mint.com, be sure to spend some time clicking the various links shown in Figure 12.15. Mint.com has a

ton of information available (for free) that is a click away. For example, if you've never invested in stocks and want to learn more, click the Investing in Stocks link, and Mint.com will give you a quick education on the basics. There are more than 25 other links indicated in Figure 12.15 that can get you up to speed on just about every aspect of your personal financial life.

When the blog opens, you are greeted with a screen similar to the one shown in Figure 12.16. I say similar because blogs (especially the good ones) continually update with new information, and the article topics you see in Figure 12.16 may be replaced with new articles by the time you read this.

FIGURE 12.16 The Mint.com blog keeps users educated with interesting financial articles.

Scroll down the page just a bit to see the complete list of topics that the blog offers, as shown in Figure 12.17. The numbers in parentheses next to each topic indicate the number of articles that exist for a particular topic. (For example, the Getting Out of Debt category has 53 articles, but check out the Frugal Living category: 208 articles!)

TOPICS

Buying a Car (5)

Getting Out of Debt (53)

Housing (34)

Retirement (15)

Saving for College (8)

Travel (24)

Student Life (35)

Becoming Wealthy (63)

Frugal Living (208)

Employment (42)

The Economy (138)

FIGURE 12.17   Articles are organized by category.

At the top of the blog you can use the Search bar to enter keywords and find articles related to your search terms. You can also click the list of Hot Topics that display across the page, as shown in Figure 12.18. These Hot Topic links take you to additional articles (not all written by Mint.com staffers) related to a topic.

Follow us: twitter | rss | daily email | facebook

Search   SEARCH

GOALS   SAVING   INVESTING   TRENDS   HOW TO   MINT UPDATES   EDUCATION   MONEY TWEETS   ANSWERS

Row of Hot Topic categories

FIGURE 12.18   Select a Hot Topic to find recent articles of interest.

When I click the Investing topic, Figure 12.19 shows a collection of articles (on the right) that might interest me, as well as a list of Popular Topics on the right that other Mint.com users are clicking and reading.

FIGURE 12.19 Hot Topics provide access to more specific topic categories and articles.

As with the Mint.com forum, you can spend hours and hours browsing through and reading all the articles that Mint.com collects on its blog. It may seem overwhelming at first, but rather than try to read it all, know it's there for you if you ever want to educate yourself on specific topics, such as mortgages, stocks and bonds, and other financial topics.

Summary

Mint.com isn't just about providing you with summaries of your financial data. The staff at Mint.com, along with other Mint.com users, are available on the site's forum when you have questions. And when you want to dive into more detailed financial reading, a quick visit to the Mint.com blog can easily turn into a long visit when you begin to educate yourself with the thousands of available articles.

Index

P

paid-off vehicles, entering value of, 70

passwords, choosing, 16

personal finance blog, 186-189

Personal Finance Blog link, 186

personal property, adding to Mint.com, 82-86

predefined goals, 135

privacy, 15

Privacy & Security link, 15

progress bar, 68-72

property, adding to Mint.com, 82-86

Q-R

Re-estimate This Goal link, 141

re-estimating goals, 141

Reimbursable tag, 47

removing. *See* deleting

reports, generating for trends, 157-158

Request That We Add Your Bank link, 39

resources

FAQs (Frequently Asked Questions), 178-181

Mint.com blog, 186-189

S

Samsung Galaxy Tab, Mint.com on, 174

Save Goal button, 144

saving goals, 144

saving money

savings values calculated by Mint.com, 7-9

spotting trends, 10

Ways to Save tab, 159-163

savings accounts

deleting, 33-35

linking to Mint.com account, 29-32

security

explained, 14-15

passwords, 16

privacy, 15

Set a Budget window, 118

Set the Timeframe section (Trends page), 154-155

Show All Alerts button, 90

Show All Goals button, 146

Sign Up button, 15-16

signing up for Mint.com, 15-16

smart phones. *See* mobile devices

sorting budgets, 130-131

Sorting By menu, 130-131

spending, tracking with Budgets tool, 128

Spending field (Budgets tool), 128

spotting trends, 10, 154-159

choosing graphs, 155-157

getting reports, 157-158

setting timeframe, 154-155

Start a New Topic page, 183

T

tablets. *See* mobile devices

tabs. *See* specific tabs

Sams**TeachYourself**

from Sams Publishing

FREE Online Edition

Your purchase of *Sams Teach Yourself Mint.com in 10 Minutes* includes access to a free online edition for 45 days through the Safari Books Online subscription service. Nearly every Sams book is available online through Safari Books Online, along with more than 5,000 other technical books and videos from publishers such as Addison-Wesley Professional, Cisco Press, Exam Cram, IBM Press, O'Reilly, Prentice Hall, and Que.

SAFARI BOOKS ONLINE allows you to search for a specific answer, cut and paste code, download chapters, and stay current with emerging technologies.

Activate your FREE Online Edition at www.informit.com/safarifree

> **STEP 1:** Enter the coupon code: RSTWNGA.

> **STEP 2:** New Safari users, complete the brief registration form. Safari subscribers, just log in.

If you have difficulty registering on Safari or accessing the online edition, please e-mail customer-service@safaribooksonline.com